Sandra Akinbolu is an experienced and approachable practitioner at 36 Group. She specialises in Immigration, Asylum and Public law and regularly lectures in related topics. Ranked as a Leading Junior by Legal 500 and Chambers & Partners, she is approachable, knowledgeable and committed to the interests of her clients.

Sandra obtained an LLB in English and European Laws from Essex University, before gaining her LLM in International Human Rights Law, with a particular specialism in refugee law. She was called to the bar in 2002, following a period of employment with the UN High Commissioner for Human Rights.

D1664208

A Practical Guide to Refugee Resettlement in the United Kingdom

A Practical Guide to Refugee Resettlement in the United Kingdom

Sandra Akinbolu,
Barrister, Middle Temple,
LLB (Hons), LLM

Law Brief Publishing

Published 2022 by Law Brief Publishing, an imprint of Law Brief Publishing Ltd
30 The Parks
Minehead
Somerset
TA24 8BT

www.lawbriefpublishing.com

Paperback: 978-1-914608-43-8

PREFACE

Refugee resettlement as a durable solution for those fleeing persecution in their home countries has been around for many years. However, little is known amongst legal practitioners in host countries like the UK about the process. As the UK left the European Union, and thus the Common European Asylum System, followed swiftly by the global pandemic and the shutdown of transport routes that it caused, increasing numbers of refugees have resorted to ever more dangerous routes to enter the United Kingdom. From a baseline of zero in 2018, more than 10,000 individuals arrived by small boat in 2022, most of whom claimed asylum. This has led to a domestic call for more "safe and legal" routes, and an increasing interest in refugee resettlement as a means of ensuring safe arrivals. The war in Ukraine, bringing the notion of conflict and large-scale population movements closer to home, has intensified the desire to know more about the process.

This book attempts to bring that knowledge together in an accessible format. It is written in autumn 2022, and is current as at 01 November 2022.

Sandra Akinbolu
November 2022

STOP PRESS – UPDATE 30/11/22:

The ongoing crisis in Afghanistan continues to produce refugees in significant numbers, and by extension applicants for resettlement in the UK and elsewhere. Successful challenges to decisions to refuse individual refugees resettlement remain rare – a great deal of deference is afforded to assessments by the Secretaries of State of the Home Department, and where appropriate, Defence. The case of *R (BAL) v Secretary of State for Defence* [2022] EWHC 2757 (Admin) is a rare example of a successful rationality challenge against such a decision.

The first Claimant had been a Judge for many years prior to the Taliban takeover of Afghanistan. His work involved a close partnership with the British Embassy in Kabul and many of the criminals he convicted, including dangerous drug producers and dealers, have been released by the Taliban. The British Embassy paid part of his salary and provided him and his family with assistance with personal protection due to the risks associated with his work. He had initially been told he would be evacuated under the ARAP scheme, but was never called forward to attend at Kabul Airport for evacuation in August 2021. This failure caused serious harm to him and his family. By June 2022, BAL and two his sons had been arrested and detained by the Taliban.

The family sought judicial review, during which the first Claimant and his wife were relocated to the UK in August 2022. Their children, all over 18 but single and remaining within the family home, were refused leave outside the Rules on the grounds that they were not themselves at risk from the Taliban, despite a Ministry of Defence assessment that they were in fact at risk. They sought judicial review on the grounds that the decision was irrational.

Steyn J agreed. He accepted that LOTR was granted only in compelling cases, but noted that DARR panel assessing the threat level had found that the risk to the children was said to be the same as their father's. namely "*Almost Certain/Highly Likely (80 to 95%) to be subject to reprisal by Taliban/Criminals*". Such a level of risk could not rationally be regarded as other than compelling (at 97). While the threat level was not determinative, it was highly probative and could only be rejected if there were cogent reasons for doing so. In the present case, the reasons for doing so, based on "absurd" credibility points and serious errors of fact were irrational, and thus the decision to refuse LOTR were quashed.

This remains a rare example of a successful challenge against refusals of this sort, but emphasises the importance of examining decisions, and the reasons for reaching them, in detail.

CONTENTS

CHAPTER ONE

WHAT IS RESETTLEMENT AND HOW DOES THE INTERNATIONAL PROCESS WORK?

International refugee law addresses the immediate recognition of refugees and the short-term protection for those fleeing situations of persecution in their home countries. It does not provide for long-term or durable solutions; that has been worked out in practice over the years. The preferred durable solution within the international community is for refugees to voluntarily return to their homes once the situation of persecution has been safely resolved, and international political will focusses on this option, both as a means of maintaining pressure on their home countries to resolve those situations and to avoid long term political and financial drains on refugee hosting countries, usually those adjacent to the home country. Nonetheless, many refugee populations remain outside from their home countries for considerable periods, and thus other durable solutions have had to be found.

Resettlement is one of the durable solutions proposed for those who have fled their countries of origin in order to seek international protection. The best definition for refugee resettlement can be found in the UNHCR Resettlement Handbook:

> "*Resettlement involves the selection and transfer of refugees from a State in which they have protection to a third State that has agreed to admit them – as refugees – with permanent residence status. The status provided ensures protection*

against refoulement and provides a resettled refugee and his/her family or dependants with access to rights similar to those enjoyed by nationals. Resettlement also carries with it the opportunity to eventually become a naturalized citizen of the resettlement country."[1]

Resettlement offers a mechanism for burden-sharing within the international community. The vast majority of refugees cross borders and remain in countries adjacent to their home country,[2] placing sometimes enormous responsibility on countries that often do not have the financial and political capital to cope. In recent years, resettlement has increasingly been portrayed as a means of reducing irregular routes of migration and combatting the trade in trafficking of persons.[3]

Resettlement goes far beyond the relocation of refugees; resettlement States commit to receiving refugees and assisting with their integration into the host country. Integration is a complex and gradual process with legal, economic, social and cultural dimensions. It imposes considerable demands on both the individual and the receiving society, which will invest funds into providing access to education and the labour market, assisting with linguistic integration and providing for medical and other needs. It requires a willingness for host communities to be welcoming and responsive to refugees and for public institutions to meet the needs of a diverse population. On the

---

[1] UNHCR Resettlement Handbook, Geneva, Revised edition July 2011 (available at http://www.unhcr.org/resettlementhandbook)

[2] UNHCR Refugee Data Finder, accessible at https://www.unhcr.org/refugee-statistics/

[3] See for example Explanatory Memorandum to the Proposal for a Regulation of The European Parliament and Of The Council establishing a Union Resettlement Framework and amending Regulation (EU) No 516/2014 of the European Parliament and the Council

part of the refugee, it involves an understanding that there will be a need to adapt to the lifestyle in the host country, without losing their cultural and ethnic identities.

The Office of the United Nations High Commissioner for Refugees [UNHCR] is the body charged by the international community with overseeing the resettlement process. It's two core objectives, of *"providing international protection"* and *"seeking permanent solutions for the problem of refugees"*, mean that the resettlement of refugees falls squarely within its mandate.[4] UNHCR notes that resettlement serves three functions: (i) resettlement is an important protection tool to meet the specific needs of refugees whose fundamental rights are at risk in the country where they sought asylum; (ii) resettlement offers refugees a long term solution by ending their displacement, and (iii) resettlement is an international responsibility sharing mechanism because it signals support for countries hosting large refugee populations.

Art 1A of the 1951 Refugee Convention defines a refugee as a person *"who is unable or unwilling to return to their country of origin owing to a well-founded fear of being persecuted for reasons of race, religion, nationality, membership of a particular social group, or political opinion."* UNHCR recognise a wider definition of refugees and supports those who are fleeing conflict or persecution. In both scenarios, to be a refugee, the person must be outside their country of nationality and in danger should they return there.

International refugee law sits within a body of international and regional human rights instruments. The right to seek asylum is recognized as a basic human right set out in the Universal Declaration

---

4   The 1950 Statute of the Office of the United Nations High Commissioner for Refugees, adopted by the General Assembly on 14 December 1950

of Human Rights.[5] The fundamental right of the refugee is not to be *refouled*, that is sent back to the country in which they fear persecution or ill-treatment.[6] However none of the international legislative instruments set out any entitlement to residence in any particular location.

Resettlement was once a popular long-term solution; in 1979, approximately five percent of the global refugee population was resettled. Since that date, numbers have declined. The UNHCR Framework for Durable Solutions for Refugees and Persons of Concern, concluded in September 2003, was the first international instrument pointing towards a greater international responsibility for refugees, and promoting greater burden sharing. Resettlement was a key part of that program but recognised as an appropriate solution mainly for individual refugees with special protection needs, made usually "*only in the absence of other options such as voluntary repatriation and local integration*".[7] Few countries have official resettlement programs, although *ad hoc* agreements are made on occasion in response to urgent needs.[8]

On average now, therefore, less than one percent of the world's refugee population benefit from resettlement. The vast majority of refugees cross borders closest to their home and remain there. This can cause destabilisation for the local communities, who suddenly have to cater for the irregular movement of large numbers of people, placing strain on water, food, housing and education systems, amongst others.

---

[5] UN General Assembly, Universal Declaration of Human Rights, 10 December 1948, 217 A (III)

[6] Convention Relating to the Status of Refugees, 28 July 1951, United Nations, Treaty Series, vol. 189, p. 137, Article 33

[7] UNHCR, Resettlement Handbook, at 2.

[8] See for example the response of the European Union to the vast displacement of people following the war in Ukraine

Refugees end up residing for lengthy periods in camps built for temporary purposes, unable to integrate into the host communities, and with no ability to make progress with their lives. In 2019, UNHCR identified 1.4 million refugees in need of resettlement.[9] Almost all of these individuals were in the Middle East or in Africa. This number was 19% higher than in 2018 and 77% higher than in 2011. 81,000 people were submitted for resettlement by the UNHCR and 56,000 people were resettled. These numbers have been diminishing since 2015.

Resettlement has the added benefit of commanding public support for the refugees in the host country and allowing States to control the entry of those in need. Those identified as refugees prior to their arrival are able to provide social, economic and financial contributions to their host State on arrival, obviating the need for expensive and often prolonged status determination procedures.

The UNHCR process

UNHCR continually seeks to increase the number of places world-wide, citing the protective functions for the refugees themselves, and the need for increased responsibility and burden sharing. However, only a small number of countries provide regular places, and those that regard resettlement as important commitment to the global community are fewer still.[10] The UNHCR resettlement handbook, first published in 1996, has been used by hundreds of UNHCR staff,

---

[9] UNHCR Resettlement Data, accessible on
   https://www.unhcr.org/uk/resettlement-data.html

[10] In its report, *Final Report: The Three-Year Strategy (2019-2021) on Resettlement and Complementary Pathways*, UNHCR note that in 2019, the last pre-pandemic year, resettlement submissions were accepted by just 29 countries. The number fell in the next 2 years.

resettlement country operatives and partner NGOs to help hundreds of thousands of refugees find new settled lives in new countries. The handbook, last revised in 2011, but regularly updated to contain the various country programs, is an essential read for anyone involved in resettlement.

UNHCR operates in most countries in which there are large refugee communities. They will seek to address the protection concerns of refugees located in that country, often by finding a solution where they are located. Where a refugee's protection concerns cannot be addressed where they are located, UNHCR may seek to resettle the refugee. The UNHCR office in the country of asylum where the refugee is located will review the case. If a refugee is identified for resettlement by UNHCR they will be referred to an appropriate resettlement country. When UNHCR submits refugees for resettlement, the resettlement country makes the final decision on whether to accept their case.

Resettlement is effected with the consent of the refugee. Art 31(2) of the Refugee Convention requires States to grant refugees the time and access to facilities to pursue resettlement options before settling on alternative long-term solutions in the host State. The includes affording the refugee time to apply for a visa or consideration within a scheme run or administered by UNHCR, suspending removal or relocation plans of the host State for a "reasonable period". Refugees should also be assisted with the process and permitted to travel to the relevant diplomatic or other offices necessary to make those arrangements.

UNHCR partners with various local and international non-governmental organisations (NGOs) to help with assessing needs and to build links with various resettlement programs. That partnership includes identifying refugees in particular need of resettlement, either because of a heightened risk, or a specific characteristic meaning resettlement is the most appropriate need for them. Such identification may take a variety of forms and may be brought to UNHCR's attention in a variety of ways, from simply flagging the case, to a more in-depth case write-up.[11] As such, in practice, referral to a particular scheme will often be done by an NGO working with the refugee community – often those providing legal, medical or psychosocial support in host camps. Referrals can also be made from legal partners in the resettlement country, either directly to bodies overseeing a particular resettlement scheme in the country of proposed resettlement, or more often to UNHCR.

NGOs conduct resettlement related assessments with refugees, often in the form of interviews, focussed on their experiences in the country of origin, details of their flight from that country, experiences in the country of asylum, opportunities for other durable solutions such as local integration or voluntary repatriation, and any immediate protection concerns and/or specific profile for resettlement consideration (e.g. women-at-risk, unaccompanied minors etc), and then referring the case to UNHCR for review, approval and onward submission to a resettlement country. Submission can be made directly to the country of proposed resettlement, subject to the specific terms of that program. NGOs can assist with identifying groups of refugees with similar backgrounds and protection needs and who might qualify for resettlement. In these cases, NGOs can document the situation of the group and their need for resettlement according to UNHCR's guidelines, and then forward information to UNHCR and/or a resettlement country for consideration.

Upon receipt of internal or external referrals of cases potentially in need of resettlement, UNHCR assesses resettlement needs of the referred cases in line with UNHCR resettlement criteria, guidelines,

---

[11] For more information, see the UNHCR-NGO Toolkit for Practical Cooperation on Resettlement

priorities and policy considerations. Once the decision has been made to submit the case for resettlement, UNHCR prepares a resettlement submission. This process includes preparing the Resettlement Registration Form (RRF) and appropriate documentation, depending on the applicable resettlement criterion. Upon reaching a final decision based on a thorough review of documentation, UNHCR submits the case to a resettlement State

UNHCR Preconditions for Resettlement Consideration

UNHCR operates a general set of conditions for individuals to be considered as eligible for resettlement, independent of the additional criteria imposed for specific schemes.[12] An applicant must have been determined to be a refugee by UNHCR – ie has gone through a status identification process; and the prospects for all durable solutions have been assessed, and resettlement is identified as the most appropriate solution. Thereafter, referrals for resettlement are considered according to 3 priority levels:

- Emergency:

  o Security and/or medical condition requires immediate removal. Ideally, there would be a seven-day maximum between the submission of an emergency case and the refugee's departure.

- Urgent:

---

[12] UNHCR Resettlement Handbook, Chapter 6

o Serious medical risks or other vulnerabilities requiring expedited resettlement within six weeks of submission.

- Normal:

    o The majority of cases without immediate medical, social or security concerns which would merit expedited processing

UNHCR operates seven categories for submission for resettlement:[13]

- Legal and/or physical protection needs, identified where there is

    o Risk of immediate or long-term threat of refoulement to the country of origin or expulsion to another country from where the refugee may be refouled; or

    o Threat of arbitrary arrest, detention or imprisonment: or

    o Threat to physical safety or human rights in the country of refuge which renders asylum untenable

- Survivors of violence and/or torture, where the individual produces evidence that they have

    o has experienced torture and/or violence either in the country of origin or the country of asylum; and

    o may have lingering physical or psychological effects from the torture or violence, although there may be no apparent physical signs or symptoms; and

---

[13] UNHCR Resettlement Handbook: Chapter 6

- could face further traumatization and/or heightened risk due to the conditions of asylum or repatriation; and

- may require medical or psychological care, support or counselling not available in the country of asylum; and

- requires resettlement to meet their specific needs

• Medical needs (very limited)

  - must provide evidence of a condition that is life-threatening, or involves an irreversible loss of functions, for which there is no accessible treatment in the country of asylum

  - identifiable and favourable treatment is available on resettlement

• Women and girls at risk, defined as those who:

  - face a precarious security or physical protection threat as a result of her gender;

  - have specific needs arising from past persecution and/or trauma;

  - face severe hardship resulting in exposure to exploitation and abuse; or

  - lack access to traditional or alternative support and protection mechanisms.

• Family reunification with family in a resettlement country

• Children and adolescents at risk

- subject to a best interests determination

- considerations of family links to host country and country of origin

- considerations of the services and support packages available are relevant

- Lack of foreseeable alternative durable solutions

  - Commonly used for group resettlement where there is a protracted crisis in the country of origin and large refugee populations causing crises in the country of asylum.

Individuals may meet one or several of the categories. The most common resettlement affects those with legal and/or physical protection needs, often combined with medical emergencies. In areas of largescale displacement, medical facilities are rarely capable of catering to severe medical conditions.

Once identified as a person in need of resettlement, UNHCR will seek to refer the individual or family to an appropriate program. UNHCR resettlement staff member will prepare and submit a Resettlement Registration Form (RRF), that includes biographical information on each person on the case, a comprehensive outline of the refugee claim and of the UNHCR determination for each adult, a detailed explanation of the need for resettlement, information on any specific needs and vulnerabilities, and any additional information including dependency assessments.

UNHCR will also identify a suitable resettlement State. Suitability considerations will include: family links, particularly those in resettlement States; UNHCR resettlement submission priority, vulnerability, and the resettlement country's average processing time and capacity for urgent processing; selection criteria and admission priorities of resettlement countries; allocation of annual quotas of resettlement States; health requirements and the availability of treatment in the resettlement country; language abilities; cultural aspects; nationality; family configuration; and, if possible: the refugee's expressed preference for a resettlement country.

UNHCR makes a referral to the resettlement State, which will then undertake its own assessment. Each State has its own procedures for making the assessment. If accepted, UNHCR works with the International Organisation for Migration (IOM) to provide medical screening, access to travel documentation and to organise travel, where possible with the assistance of the resettlement country. IOM will also provide support with post-arrival integration where needed.

<u>State Selection</u>

Actual resettlement depends on the identification of a suitable resettlement country, and the willingness of the country to accept the referral, in accordance with its own policies and laws. Each case must include a principal applicant who has been identified as a refugee, and meet the resettlement needs identified in accordance with the identification categories above.[14] Thereafter, UNHCR will consider a number of factors, in order to determine which of the various global resettlement schemes is appropriate for the particular family. Those factors will include:[15]

- family links, particularly those in resettlement States;

---

[14] UNHCR Resettlement Handbook, Chapter 7.6

[15] UNHCR Resettlement Handbook, Chapter 7.6

- resettlement submission priority, vulnerability, and the resettlement country's average processing time and capacity for urgent processing;

- selection criteria and admission priorities of resettlement countries;

- allocation of annual quotas of resettlement States;

- health requirements/availability of treatment;

- language abilities;

- cultural aspects;

- nationality;

- family configuration; and, if possible:

- the refugee's expressed preference for a resettlement country

Resettlement countries consider referrals usually on the basis of the written referral, and do not interview the refugee personally. Some States will identify a particular refugee population or region from which they will accept referrals; others leave it to UNHCR to determine. UNHCR may also approach countries without a specific resettlement scheme, as some States accept resettled refugees on an *ad hoc* basis. A useful list of the various country programs can be found on the Country Chapters of the UNHCR Handbook.

Some States undergo selection missions, allowing them to conduct assessments and gain familiarity with the context in which a particular refugee population is living. Such missions are planned in conjunction with UNHCR and usually require an agreement ahead of time as to the proposed number of families the mission will accept. State may conduct interviews with selected families, which allows family members to provide any such additional information as they feel necessary. States may request additional information but UNHCR may only disclose such information as is necessary, in conjunction with its own *Confidentiality Guidelines*.[16]

Decisions by the resettlement country will be communicated to the UNHCR field office from which the referral has come. It is then for the UNHCR staff to inform the refugee family of that decision. Where the decision is a positive decision, the next step is make arrangement for departure, and UNHCR will collaborate with the IOM and governments in both the host States and the resettlement country to ensure that pre-departure preparation are completed. If the decision is a rejection, the reasons should be carefully considered, and UNHCR will determine whether the case warrant a resubmission or not. That in turn will be communicated with the refugee family, who have a right to be provided with the reasons for the rejection. Where there is further information or the circumstances change, UNHCR may approach the resettlement country and request a review. In the alternative, UNHCR may consider resubmitting the application to a different resettlement State, although given the disparity in numbers seeking resettlement and places offered, that is rare.[17]

On occasion, a decision will be made to accept the referral on behalf of some members of a family, and not others. UNHCR will normally seek to advocate in favour of keeping the family together but if the resettlement country refuses to reconsider, UNHCR will normally advise the family to withdraw their application and try another country. Refugee families may choose to take the pragmatic step of

---

[16] UNHCR, Confidentiality Guidelines, 1 August 2001

[17] For more detail, see UNHCR, Guidelines on the Resubmission of Resettlement Cases, June 2011

splitting the family, and in such cases, UNHCR provides some counselling in making that decision.

Resettlement is an international commitment, requiring global cooperation and organisation. UNHCR lies at the heart of the movements, integral both to the refugee status determination procedure, and the identification and referral of relevant refugees to suitable programs. Most resettlement countries, including the UK, work closely with UNHCR and thus it is vital that those working with resettled refugees understand the processes adopted.

CHAPTER TWO

UK PRACTICE
IN GENERAL

The UK has a long and proud history of commitment to refugee resettlement. In 1956, after Soviet tanks had rolled into Budapest, the UK resettled approximately 11,000 Hungarian refugees in a matter of months. In 1972, after Idi Amin gave them 90 days to leave, the UK resettled nearly 30,000 Ugandan Asian refugees. Between 1979 and 1983, the UK resettled around 16,000 Vietnamese refugees. From August 2016 to August 2022, the UK resettled 26,143 people, the majority of whom were Syrian nationals. Refugee communities, welcomed in this way, provide valuable cultural, financial and social additions to the UK.

The UK is one of few countries worldwide that has an established global resettlement program. Its resettlement schemes represent the only routes by which refugees in need of protection may lawfully enter the United Kingdom in accordance with domestic legal policy.

Access to the scheme remains co-ordinated by the Home Office in conjunction with UNHCR. The UK works very closely with the UNHCR to identify refugees in need of resettlement. Whilst the UK sets the criteria for eligibility in each scheme, it generally leaves it to UNHCR to identify those in need of resettlement and those who would fit best within each scheme. In practice, this means that Palestinians who are supported by UNRWA are ineligible for consideration under any of the UK's main resettlement schemes, although they may fall for consideration under the family reunion rules.[18]

Ordinarily, individuals and families cannot access the UK's resettlement schemes until UNHCR has undergone the status determination process in the country of asylum. This obviates the need for the UK to undertake a separate refugee status definition process, meaning individuals resettled are accepted as refugees on arrival.[19] Although UNHCR operates a wider definition of who is a refugee, and in a status determination process conducted in the UK, holding UNHCR's refugee status documentation has persuasive, but not binding authority,[20] for the purposes of access to the resettlement program, the UK will accept that those in possession of a UNHCR approved refugee ID document is a refugee. The UK may determine an annual quota of resettled refugees, having considered the resources available. It then ensures that UNHCR is aware of the annual number. Where parallel schemes are running, this may lead to a lower number of refugees taken under the three main schemes; rarely is the total number of those received increased.

We look at the detailed criteria for eligibility on the various programs in the next Chapter. The UK now operates three main schemes, the

---

[18] In *Turani & Anor v Secretary of State for the Home Department* [2021] EWCA Civ 348, [2021] 1 WLR 5793, the Court of Appeal found that the drafters of the various resettlement schemes had not in fact given any consideration to the effect on those protected by United Nations Relief and Works Agency, the body responsible for the assistance of Palestinians in Lebanon, Jordan, Syria the West Bank and Gaza. However, their exclusion from the scheme was not discriminatory because the Equality Act 2010 had no extra-territorial effect.

[19] See for example *ST & Anor v The Secretary of State for the Home Department* [2014] EWCA Civ 188, *per* McCombe LJ at 46

[20] *IA v The Secretary of State for the Home Department (Scotland)* [2014] UKSC 6, *per* Lord Kerr

UK Resettlement Scheme, the Community Sponsorship Scheme and the Mandate Resettlement Scheme, plus a family reunion route. From time to time, the UK will additionally operate specific schemes to combat particular situations.[21] Such schemes follow the general principles of the broad resettlement policy but reflect the risks facing particular refugee populations and seek to speed up the resettlement process.

Dublin III

The UK was a signatory to the Dublin III Regulation,[22] a significant part of the "Common European Asylum System", which provides a system of responsibility and burden sharing throughout the European Union. The Dublin procedure sets a hierarchy for determining which state should be responsible for processing an asylum application, including a procedure prioritising family reunion for those seeking asylum and governing transfer processes and timescales. Significant numbers of people were thus transferred across Europe in line with criteria set up, allowing for those seeking asylum to be processed in the country deemed most appropriate to do so. A key provision allowed those with families resident in one of the European countries, particularly unaccompanied minors, to be transferred to join them, before any status determination took place. With the UK's withdrawal

---

21 At the time of writing, bespoke schemes for Afghan nationals, Ukraine nationals and British Nationals (Overseas) with a connection to Hong Kong are running, in parallel to the 3 main schemes. Schemes set up to assist specifically with resettlement from Syria closed in 2021, although Syrian nationals form the majority of those benefiting from the UKRS

22 Regulation (EU) No 604/2013 of the European Parliament and of the Council of 26 June 2013 establishing the criteria and mechanisms for determining the Member State responsible for examining an application for international protection lodged in one of the Member States by a third-country national or a stateless person (recast)

from the EU on 31 December 2020, all obligations under the Dublin procedure ceased – the UK did not want to retain its commitments thereunder. Neither the UK-EU Political Declaration, nor the EU's draft text for a new partnership agreement with the UK, specifically identified asylum, unaccompanied children, or readmissions as areas for future agreement or co-operation.

The impact of withdrawal from the Dublin procedure has been the loss of previously established lawful routes of entry, particularly the route for reuniting family members seeking asylum. The UK has similarly lost the power to return those seeking asylum to countries within the EU that the UK considers more appropriate to process the asylum claim. The UK has attempted to agree bilateral agreements with various EU States.[23]

Procedure

Although each scheme has slightly different criteria, the procedure applicable for accessing the main schemes is similar for all. UNHCR makes status determination and considers the individual or group in accordance with its own criteria (see Chapter 1). Thereafter, UNHCR will determine whether resettlement is in fact the appropriate durable solution, and if so, will consider the various global resettlement schemes to determine which is best suited to the individual's needs. This process can be aided by the assistance of NGO partners, who are

---

[23] On 30 April 2020, the UK signed a strategic action plan "*to deepen cooperation on migration*". The agreement includes a commitment to ensure a smooth family reunification program, with a particular emphasis on the needs of unaccompanied children eligible under s.67 of the Immigration Act 2016 and the Dublin III Regulation, whilst the UK remained bound by it. No other agreement had been signed by October 2022.

able to complete referral forms, highlighting the particular needs of individual refugees.

If UNHCR determines that an individual or group should be referred, they complete the UK Resettlement Registration Form (RRF) which is submitted to the UK's casework team. That team assesses the referral in accordance with the UK's eligibility criteria and conducts the necessary security checks. All security checks are conducted in line with the criteria in Art 1F of the Refugee Convention, and thus the UK team will consider whether individuals have been involved in or linked with terrorism, war crimes, crimes against humanity or whether they are guilty of serious non-political crimes.[24]

The UK will then conduct an interview with family members or sponsors in the UK, if any, to ascertain the level of support necessary. The application is then considered based on that interview, the RRF and any other information available regarding both the refugee and their family members in the UK. Decision-making is usually relatively swift. The UK currently has no emergency procedure, and thus those identified by UNHCR as requiring urgent resettlement will rarely be eligible for the UK's schemes.

Once a referral has been accepted, the UK will notify UNHCR, who in turn will notify the individual or family involved. The UK will work closely with the International Organisation for Migration (IOM) to obtain travel assistance, health assessment and documents for those accepted on the scheme. The IOM, together with UNHCR will conduct health screening in the host country to ensure appropriate care can be arranged on arrival and to ensure those with tuberculosis

---

[24] For examples of offences which the UK considers will lead to refusal, please see the API *Exclusion under Article 1F of the Refugee Convention*.

and other infectious diseases are not resettled until their condition poses minimal harm.

Those accepted on the scheme are then required to undertake the biometric registration process and will be issued with a visa providing them with leave to enter, outside the rules, for 6 months. IOM will use those visas to obtain an exit permit, if needed, from their host country, and they will then be able to travel, escorted by an IOM representative. Where emergency travel documents are necessary, those will normally be provided by the UK.

Since October 2021, all resettled refugees are granted Indefinite Leave to Remain (ILR) on arrival. Those resettled before that date are eligible to apply for indefinite leave to remain at no further cost.

Refugees aged 14 and above who are being resettled through the UKRS and Community Sponsorship Scheme are invited to attend a 3-day pre-departure cultural orientation session delivered by IOM which gives them the opportunity to acquire information they will need when they arrive in the UK.

Rights of Resettled Refugees

A key commitment in any resettlement program is the integration process after arrival. In the UK, the annual quota is fixed in conjunction with the local authorities. Resettled refugee families are met by the responsible sponsor, and assisted with settlement into the community in which they are placed. Local authorities oversee that process, and are provided with additional funding to do so.

Refugees arriving are issued with a biometric residence card (BRP). This includes all children, irrespective of age. This will enable them to prove their identity and immigration status, access housing and public funds, or register for work. Those over 16 will have been assigned a national insurance number, which will be included on the BRP on arrival.

Resettled refugees have an immediate right to work and access benefits, including housing. How that is funded depends on the particular scheme through which they have arrived. Local authorities working within the schemes will have been provided with funding to ensure that refugees are supported at least during the first 12 months. Much of that support is directed in assisting resettled refugees access the job market and public services. Those who enter through the UKRS scheme are entitled to local authority sourced housing, provided through private landlords, and those on the Community Sponsorship scheme will have their housing supported by the sponsorship group for 24 months.

All refugees can access mainstream education. Children under 18 must attend school and are able to do so without further cost. Adults needing English language education should receive a minimum of eight hours English language tuition, where needed, for the first twelve months. Resettled refugees are eligible for home fee status for tuition fees in England, Wales and Northern Ireland. In Scotland, further/higher education is free for students resettled through the UK's resettlement schemes who have been ordinarily resident in the UK at all times since being granted leave to remain and are ordinarily resident in Scotland on the date they start the course. Refugee students will also be eligible for student finance assistance, subject to the relevant criteria of each program.[25]

---

25 For more on student financing, please visit UKCISA (https://www.ukcisa.org.uk/Information--Advice/Fees-and-Money/Government-Student-Support#layer-6193) or the Refugee Education UK website, (https://www.reuk.org/hefaq-refugee-hp-calais-stateless-67)

Resettled refugees are eligible for a Refugee Convention travel document and are advised not to travel on their national passports after entry, as this may affect their refugee status.[26] They are permitted to travel, although most countries require visas to do so, and travel to the country of origin is likely to lead to an assertion that their need for international protection has ceased.[27] In such circumstances, consideration will be given as to whether to revoke their refugee status.

Loss of protection status

Resettled refugees are subject to the same protections and duties as refugees and thus may lose their refugee status if they commit a serious criminal offence. A serious criminal offence in considered to be one which attracts a sentence of two years imprisonment.[28] In the event of being notified of criminality, the Secretary of State will review the resettled refugee's status and consider whether they constitute a danger to the community. The review will initially review eligibility to refugee status, and then consider whether they can remain in the UK.

As a general rule, the criminal sentence suffices to give rise to the presumption that the person constitutes a danger to the public. This presumption is rebuttable, but the individual bears the burden to

---

[26] Those applying for national passports are likely to have their status reviewed, in line with the cessation provisions. For more, please see the API *Revocation of protection status*

[27] Art 1C Refugee Convention.

[28] S.72(2) Nationality, Immigration and Asylum Act 2002 defines a particularly serious crime. The two years refers to immediate criminal sentences and includes detention in institutions other than prisons, such as Young Offenders Institutions of in hospital.

proving that they do not present a danger, despite the conviction.[29] A person found to have committed a particularly serious crime and to pose a danger to the community will have their refugee status revoked.

If the individual continues to face a risk if returned to their home country despite losing their refugee status, or there are other sufficiently strong human rights concerns mitigating against expulsion (eg. strong family or medical needs), their indefinite leave to remain will be revoked and replaced with a more limited form of leave to remain. The Secretary of State may impose additional condition, depending on the nature of the risk posed, designed to restrict movement and protect the public.

As resettled refugees are now granted indefinite leave to remain on arrival, they will be eligible to naturalise after five years. Children who are reaching the end of the minority, or for whom there are particular needs, may be eligible to register as British citizens sooner.[30] Once naturalised or registered as a British citizen, the individual is no longer a resettled refugee and ceases to be eligible for the protections afforded to such persons, although will be entitled to the full panoply of rights afforded as a citizen.

---

[29] *EN (Serbia) v Secretary of State for the Home Department & Anor* [2009] EWCA Civ 630, [2010] 3 WLR 182

[30] See the naturalisation Guidance – *Registration as a British citizen: children*

CHAPTER THREE

CURRENT UK RESETTLEMENT SCHEMES

The UK operates 3 main schemes, the UK Resettlement Scheme, the Community Sponsorship Scheme and the Mandate Resettlement Scheme. This chapter will look at the criteria for inclusion within each and the process in which they operate.

The UK Resettlement Scheme (UKRS)

The UKRS is now the UK's main resettlement scheme, delivered in partnership with local authorities and funded by the Home Office. The scheme opened in March 2021, with the stated purpose to "*to resettle vulnerable refugees in need of protection from a range of regions of conflict and instability across the globe*".[31] It consolidated three previous schemes, the Vulnerable Persons' Resettlement Scheme (VPRS), the Vulnerable Children's Resettlement Scheme (VCRS) and the gateway protection programme, all of which had had a limited geographical remit, into one global scheme. Access to this scheme is theoretically available to recognised refugees around the world, although in practice the UK predominantly works with UNHCR partners in specific

---

[31] UK Resettlement policy. The scheme initially prioritised those coming from the Middle East and North African region, although has since broadened its scope.

refugee-hosting countries. As with its predecessors, Palestinian refugees supported by UNRWA remain excluded from access.[32]

The numbers accepted through this scheme are determined annually, depending on local authorities' capacity for accommodating refugees. Refugees are matched with a local authority, who will then take responsibility for receiving, housing and supporting those resettled in their community with practical integration support.

The scheme incorporates the resettlement of unaccompanied children. One of its predecessors, VCRS, was launched in April 2016 and closed to new arrivals on 25 February 2021. The VCRS was specifically designed to resettle vulnerable refugee children and their families from the Middle East and North Africa region. The UKRS has a broader remit, having no geographic limitations and thus children and families fleeing persecution and in need of resettlement from all parts of the globe can be accommodated within the scheme. If UNHCR determine that resettlement is in the best interests of an unaccompanied child, they can be considered within the UKRS.

The UKRS adopts the UNHCR eligibility criteria, and therefore those eligible for resettlement under the scheme fall into the seven categories described in Chapter 1:

- Legal and/or Physical Protection Needs;

- Survivors of Violence and/or Torture;

---

[32] See Chapter 2, above, and *Turani & Anor v Secretary of State for the Home Department* [2021] EWCA Civ 348, [2021] 1 WLR 5793

- Medical Needs (although in practice since the UK does not currently have an urgent procedure, those meeting UNHCR's definition are unlikely to be referred to the UK);

- Women and Girls at Risk;

- Family Reunification;

- Children and Adolescents at Risk;

- Lack of Foreseeable Alternative Durable Solutions.

Individuals may not apply directly to the UK for consideration within the scheme although they may request that UNHCR make the referral to the UK. Those with family or cultural links to the UK will be prioritised.

Local authorities commit to meeting the resettled refugee at the airport, and ensuring that they are housed in adequately furnished properties for the first 12 months. The local authority provide support to access services, including utilities, education and health, and refugees are provided with a caseworker from the local authority to ensure the transition is smooth.

Community Sponsorship Scheme

The UK's Community Sponsorship program is based on a program established in Canada over 40 years ago, allowing community groups, religious organisations and other civil society organisations to play a greater role in refugee resettlement. Whilst the Canadian model was largely based around family reunion and refugee groups in the host countries identifying and supporting known individuals, the UK model allows groups to host refugee families, previously unknown to the group, and take responsibility for welcoming, supporting and helping them integrate into UK society. Although the program has been in place since 2016, the scheme gained increased popularity following the Afghan crisis and the war in Ukraine.

A community group must be registered and approved by the Home Office. Thereafter, it will work with the local authority and refugee family, committing to supporting the family in their first year in the UK. The group will be responsible for housing and financial support, enabling the refugee family to learn English, access schools, benefits, healthcare and employment, and will welcome them into the community into which the refugee family will join. Groups often play a significant role in the families lives, ensuring that families have access to clothing, are given proper orientation in the community hosting them, and providing direct, friendly links with vulnerable families.

The program is run together with Reset, a charity formed in 2018 to help grow the scheme.[33] The charity runs training sessions for community groups and local authorities and provides ongoing support and information. It is funded by the Home Office and in practice, delivery of the scheme is managed through Reset.

The criteria for eligibility for the refugee family is largely identical to that above. UNHCR will identify suitable refugee families, in line with their own criteria, and refer them to the UK for approval. The scheme initially focussed on resettling those from the Middle East and North Africa region who have waited longest for resettlement but has developed a broader scope over time and since September 2021, has included Afghan refugees fleeing the recent upheaval. Refugee families are identified by the Home Office, in conjunction with UNHCR. While a community group can refuse the particular family, and should consider carefully whether they can properly meet the needs of the

---

[33] https://resetuk.org/

refugee family referred, there is no real facility for sponsoring known refugees through this scheme.

To become a community sponsor, the group must first register for charity status, either independently or in partnership with existing charities. The group must appoint a lead sponsor, a person or group who in practice will be responsible for ensuring delivery of the sponsorship agreement, and who will act as guarantor for the group. The lead sponsor will liaise with the Home office and will assist with any problems, should the need arise. Reset coordinate a Lead Sponsorship Network, a group of approved lead sponsors who may take responsibility for new community groups.

The group will then apply for approval to the Home Office through their lead sponsor. The group must show that they have sufficient resources to support a resettled family, set out a credible and acceptable plan for supporting that family, a suitable safeguarding policy and pass fairly rigorous security checks, to ensure they do not present a danger to the resettled family.[34] In general, the application will take place after a fundraising process, to ensure that the Community group has sufficient funds. The commitment needed is to support the resettled refugee in all their needs for twelve months, and with housing for a minimum of two years. Housing does not necessarily need to have been secured at this stage, although the plan must show that the group has given thought to the accommodation situation.

Applications can be sent to the Home Office for approval in principle, allowing the group to move through the application process without making any legally binding commitment to any property. However,

---

[34] For all the guidance notes, see the Community Sponsor website (https://www.gov.uk/government/publications/apply-for-full-community-sponsorship/community-sponsorship-guidance-for-prospective-sponsors) and details on the Reset website

for the application to be finalised, the group must show that a property has been secured and that there is a minimum of £9,000 available to provide support.

Community groups will need to work with the local authority in which they are based. The local authority will be responsible for ensuring that the group has adequate safeguarding measures and the group will work with the local authority to connect the resettled refugee with relevant services. The local authority will be asked to view the property to ensure suitability and will be involved in the pre-approval meeting with the Home Office and the community group, to discuss the details of the application.

Once the referral is made, things move very quickly. The community group will be asked to accept the referral within 5 days of the family being allocated, and the Home Office will then arrange flights, usually within six to twelve weeks. The community group will meet the resettled family at the airport, and take responsibility for their settlement there. The Home Office requests ongoing record-keeping and monitoring information and Reset will arrange post-arrival meetings to provide additional support.

Mandate Resettlement Scheme

The Mandate Scheme is the oldest of the current resettlement schemes, having been in place since 1995. However, it is little known, and grossly underused. Fewer than 100 refugees were resettled under this scheme between 2015 and 2020.[35] The UK has no quota for this

---

[35] Home Office Migration Statistics,
https://www.gov.uk/government/collections/migration-statistics

category, and it is open to refugees from any part of the world, if they have been referred by UNHCR.

Unlike other resettlement schemes, the Mandate scheme is designed to accommodate known individuals. It is applicable to those who have close family member settled in the UK or in a route that will lead to settlement. The UK sponsor need not be a refugee or hold humanitarian protection status; a sponsor may be in the UK in any settled category or category leading to settlement. This therefore allows anyone lawfully resident in the UK to petition, through UNHCR, for the resettlement of family members residing outside of their country of origin. The refugee seeking resettlement must have been recognized as a refugee by UNHCR and meet UNHCR's criteria for resettlement.[36] Those eligible are the minor child, spouse, or parent or grandparent aged over sixty-five. Wider family can be considered in exceptional circumstances, where they are dependent on the UK sponsor and subject to their current living conditions.[37]

Applications are assessed on case-by-case basis. The refugee must have undergone the status determination process in the host country first, and should alert UNHCR, or the supporting NGO, to the presence of a relevant sponsor in the UK. The sponsor can assist in the process, but all initial steps will take place outside of the UK. UNHCR will make the referral to the UK, who in turn will verify both the sponsor's position and the need for the refugee to resettle.

---

[36] See Chapter 1

[37] The Court of Appeal has accepted that the SSHD is entitled to keep absolute flexibility on the interpretation of exceptional circumstances (*Per McCombe LJ, ST & Anor v Secretary of State for the Home Department* [2014] EWCA Civ 188) As such, the Secretary of State was entitled to assess exceptionality in comparison with other refugees living in the host country.

The sponsor will undertake to provide accommodation and financial support and must provide evidence that they are capable of doing so. The Home Office may fund travel if the individual cannot afford to do so and the medical costs incurred by the International Organization for Migration (IOM), but no funding is provided after a refugee arrives in the UK. However, the refugee will be granted Indefinite Leave to Remain on arrival and thus is able to access mainstream support services, as well as seek employment in any capacity.

CHAPTER FOUR

COUNTRY SPECIFIC SCHEMES

In response to specific emergencies, the UK has created routes of entry for specific categories of persons. Each scheme works slightly differently, some follow the traditional route requiring referrals, others enable individuals to apply directly to the UK for consideration. These policies are subject to change, depending on global need.

Afghanistan

The UK has operated a number of resettlement schemes to recognise the risks to those who have worked with British armed forces in Afghanistan, who often find themselves the target of reprisals. The UK's operations in Afghanistan officially began on 1 October 2001, and families who have worked with the UK since then have regularly been exposed to risks. The withdrawal of the international armed forces and the arrival of the Taliban in Kabul in August 2022 led to the further displacement of people, and further categories of persons deemed at risk as the government of Afghanistan began its crackdown on opponents. As at time of writing, there are three schemes, which are each subdivided into various categories, with slightly different qualification and application processes. Each is dealt with below.

Afghan Relocations and Assistance Policy

The Afghan Relocations and Assistance Policy (ARAP) was launched in April 2021 to provide relocation opportunities for those who had been locally engaged with UK armed forces and services in Afghanistan. ARAP replaced a previous scheme known as the Intimidation Policy, which was established in 2010 to protect Afghan staff working with the British who faced threats to their safety, relocating them to the UK only in the most serious cases. The policy initially allowed for a fairly broad case-by-case assessment of the individual need for resettlement, based on referral by UK government units of employees deemed at risk. The criteria for eligibility were narrowed considerably in December 2021, when protections were brought into the Immigration Rules,[38] making the application process both clearer and narrower. This remains a scheme primarily aimed at locally engaged staff, although it also acknowledges the importance of work carried out by individual Afghans alongside the UK government.[39]

The ARAP scheme now subdivides applicants into three categories:

- Category one: high and imminent risk of threat to life.[40] The individual must have been directly employed by a UK government department and face the high risk as a result of that employment.

---

[38] Para. 276BB3-5, inserted by HC 913

[39] *Per* Lang J, *R (S) v Secretary of State for Foreign and Commonwealth and Development Affairs and Ors* and *R (AZ) v Secretary of State for the Home Department and Ors* [2022] EWHC 1402 (Admin), at §106

[40] Para. 276BB3

- Category two: former employees eligible for relocation.[41] This group comprises those who were directly employed by a UK government department, or those who were contracted to provide linguistic services in support of the UK's Armed Forces. They must show that he nature of the role in which the person was employed was such that the UK's operations in Afghanistan would have been materially less efficient or materially less successful if a role or roles of that nature had not been performed. They must also show that they have been publicly recognised as having performed that role and that recognition has created a safety risk.

- Category three: special cases.[42] Individuals must show that they were directly employed in Afghanistan, provided goods or services in Afghanistan under contract to, or worked in Afghanistan alongside a UK government department. Their role must have contributed to the UK's military or security operations and have cause the individual to face an elevated risk of being targeted. Alternatively, the individual may show that they hold information which would cause a risk to the UK's interests if disclosed.

Eligibility is initially assessed by the relevant government department sponsoring the application, who will assess the work undertaken by the principal application against the criteria set out above. Reference will then be made to the Defence Afghan Relocation and Resettlement team (DARR) in the Ministry of Defence to approve the application.

---

[41] Para 276BB4

[42] Para 276BB5. This has been held to include some Afghan Judges, who in worked in courts supported by the UK either logistically or through training and mentoring.

Once the initial eligibility criteria are approved, an application will be made under the Immigration Rules.

Each of the principal applicants must be an adult and an Afghan citizen. Applicants may bring dependent family members, provided they are included in the application form at the time of application. Dependent family members include partners and minor children, provided that the relationships are subsisting and, in the case of children, they have not formed an independent life.[43]

Applications are now made online through the specified form and can be made from any country, including Afghanistan. Although the guidance documents still require an applicant to register biometrics in order for the application to be complete, that requirement has been found to be unlawful,[44] and in practice, those applying from Afghanistan are able to request a waiver of the requirement until after entry. If successful, applicants will be granted indefinite leave to remain as a refugee.

Afghanistan Locally Employed Staff Ex-Gratia Scheme

The Afghanistan Locally Employed Staff Ex-Gratia Scheme has been in place since 2013 and applies to those who were employed for at least 12 months, and were either made redundant or resigned on or after 1 May 2006. Employment must have been with an UK government department, and the applicant must be the beneficiary of an ex-gratia redundancy or resignation package confirming that they worked on the front-line in an exposed role, mostly in Helmand province. The scheme was designed to provide support, including but

---

[43] Para 276Bj1-276BQ1

[44] *KA & Ors, R (On the Application Of) v Secretary of State for the Home Department & Ors* (Rev1) [2022] EWHC 2473 (Admin)

not always, the opportunity to relocate to the UK where the individual and their family were in danger. Applicants had to choose one of a financial package of support, a training package or relocation to the UK, but could not accept more than one.

Previously set out in policy, this scheme was brought into the immigration rules in June 2022.[45] The Rules now confirm that the scheme would close to new applicants on 30 November 2022. Applicants were granted limited leave to enter on application, and once in the UK are able to apply for indefinite leave to remain. Applications are free of charge.

Afghan Citizens Resettlement Scheme

The Afghan Citizens Resettlement Scheme (ACRS), announced in August 2021, formally opened in January 2022, but only began accepting external referrals in June 2022. The scheme was initially focussed inwards, stretching the definition of resettlement by incorporating only those Afghans already evacuated under Operation Pitting and in the UK, providing a legal basis for recognising those individuals as refugees. Two further referral pathways were opened on 20 June 2022. The UK aims to resettle 20,000 Afghans, with 5,000 being resettled in the first year of operation.

The ACRS officially has three pathways:[46] Pathway one is effectively a catch-all for those who were evacuated last August 2021 and who did not qualify for leave under the previous Afghan Relocations and Assistance Policy but were allocated places under the new scheme. It includes those who were called to be evacuated in August 2021 but

---

[45] Para. 276BB6, inserted by HC913.

[46] Guidance: *Afghan citizens resettlement scheme*
   (https://www.gov.uk/guidance/afghan-citizens-resettlement-scheme)

were unable to board the planes. Operation Pitting, set up by the UK armed forces to evacuate British citizens and high risk locally engaged staff and their family members, brought approximately 2,000 Afghan citizens to the UK in 2021. Further numbers arrived in the following months. Those unable to board the planes are able to apply directly to the UK with proof of the letters calling them to take their place.

Pathway two reflects a more traditional resettlement route. It is open to those identified as refugees by UNHCR, living in refugee camps outside of Afghanistan and referred. UNHCR will refer individuals in accordance with their standard resettlement submission criteria (see Chapter one), which are based on an assessment of protection needs and vulnerabilities. Priority

Pathway three is open to those at risk who supported the UK and international community effort in Afghanistan, as well as those who are particularly vulnerable, such as women and girls at risk and members of minority groups. It is initially planned that the beneficiaries will be British Council and GardaWorld contractors and Alumni of the Afghanistan Chevening scholarship, who supported the UK and international community's operations in Afghanistan. British Council contractors includes *individuals who were contracted to take on regular and public-facing roles, providing services or benefits to beneficiaries on behalf of the British Council, and who were therefore closely associated with delivering the UK government's mission in Afghanistan.* GardaWorld contractors are those employed after July 2020 for at least three months. Those in a more external role, including accountants, recruiters those servicing machinery, are excluded from the scheme.

Eligible individuals were able to submit expressions of interest directly or through the relevant organisation, together with their family members who are dependent on them.[47] They are advised to raise any applicable risk factors and highlight the role played, and any further compelling circumstances. The pathway has a total cap of 1,500 places available for the first year and had a limited window for application.

Ukraine

The unexpected invasion of Ukraine by the Russian army in March 2022 led to the fastest and one of the largest displacements of people since World War II and the first European refugee crisis since the Balkan wars of the early 1990s. 7,751,169 refugees were registered across Europe between March and October 2022, with a further 4,426,745 granted some form of temporary or complementary protection.[48] Most were registered in countries bordering west Ukraine. The European Union opened its borders to Ukrainian nationals and the UK agreed to help resettle some of those in need, to alleviate the pressures on the border countries.

The UK announced two schemes to help Ukrainian nationals fleeing the conflict. Neither takes the form of the traditional resettlement route, and thus UNHCR plays not part in their operation.

---

[47] For more information see the Home Office guidance document, *Afghan Citizens Resettlement Scheme Pathway 3: eligibility for British Council and GardaWorld contractors and Chevening Alumni* (https://www.gov.uk/guidance/afghan-citizens-resettlement-scheme-pathway-3-eligibility-for-british-council-and-gardaworld-contractors-and-chevening-alumni)

[48] UNHCR data portal: *Ukraine Refugee situation* (https://data.unhcr.org/en/situations/ukraine) accessed 30 October 2022

Ukraine Family Scheme

The Ukraine Family Scheme, set out in Appendix Ukraine to the Immigration Rules, allows applicants to join their family members in the UK.[49] It was opened to those already visiting family in the UK, to allow them to extend visas. The scheme opened to those who are nationals of Ukraine and/or their immediate family member (spouse, civil partner, unmarried partner or minor child) who had been residing in Ukraine prior to 1 January 2022 with a family member legally resident in the UK. The UK-based family member must be British, hold ILR, refugee or humanitarian protection status, or pre-settled status as a result of residence in the UK prior to 1 January 2021. To be eligible, the applicant must be related to the UK-based sponsor as an immediate family member, including fiancé(e)s or as an extended family members. Extended family members are those who had a relevant relationship before 1 January 2022 and includes:

- parent (if the UK-based sponsor is over 18)

- child who is over 18

- grandparent

- grandchild or your partner's grandchild

- brother or sister

- aunt or uncle

- niece or nephew

---

[49] Appendix Ukraine, inserted into the Immigration Rules by HC 1220. See also guidance document *Ukraine Family Scheme Visa* (https://www.gov.uk/guidance/apply-for-a-ukraine-family-scheme-visa)

- cousin

- mother-in-law or father-in-law

- grandparent-in-law

- brother-in-law or sister-in-law

Other family members are considered in exceptional circumstances and in accordance with the UK's obligations under Article 8 ECHR.

Applications made from those outside of the country, whether in Ukraine or elsewhere, are made online. Applicants who are Ukrainian nationals and hold a valid, unexpired Ukraine passport will have their biometrics registered after entry, but those who do not hold a Ukrainian passport must attend an appointment at a visa application centre (VAC) to register their biometrics. Applications made in-country are also made online and attendance at a UK visa and citizenship application service point is mandatory. Applications are free of charge, but subject to identity and security checks.

On arrival, the individual or family will be given 3 years leave to remain. Individuals are permitted access to public funds and are able to work, access education and support. Importantly, individuals are not recognised as refugees on entry, they undergo no status determination, either in the UK or outside, which means they are not entitled to a Refugee Convention travel document but are able to travel to Ukraine without fear of losing their entitlement to remain in the UK.

Homes for Ukraine Scheme

The Ukraine Sponsorship Scheme (Homes for Ukraine) was set up as a fast-track version of the Community Sponsorship scheme. Individuals, charities business and community and faith groups are able to volunteer to provide a home to Ukrainian nationals and their family members. The scheme allows sponsors to house either persons they know, or to offer to house unknown people fleeing the conflict.

Sponsors must be adults lawfully resident in the UK who are able to provide suitable accommodation for a minimum of six months.[50] The Home office conducts rigorous security checks, and the local authority will examine the housing and living arrangements to ensure the safety of all concerned. Sponsorship may not be linked to conditions to work. Sponsors are not expected to meet any additional costs but should be able to help the new arrivals adapt to the community in which they are now hosted. The local authority will monitor the placement and will provide help with registering for schooling, access to benefits and advice on medical support.

The Scottish[51] and Welsh[52] governments have devolved government sponsorship, allowing them to sponsor individuals and families directly, providing housing, access to education and financial support. Applicants applying through the online system may elect the Scottish or Welsh governments as their sponsor. Accommodation is provided through local volunteers for a minimum of 3 months, after which applicants are aided to find more permanent homes. The Welsh

---

[50] Homes for Ukraine: sponsor guidance
(https://www.gov.uk/guidance/homes-for-ukraine-sponsor-guidance)

[51] The Scottish Super Sponsor Scheme, accessible through
https://www.mygov.scot/visa-sponsorship-ukrainians-scotland. This route was temporarily paused on 13 July 2022

[52] The Super Sponsor scheme, accessible on https://sanctuary.gov.wales/super

authorities additionally provide free travel throughout Wales for the first six months.

Applications may only be made from outside the UK and are made online. Applicants must be Ukrainian nationals or their non-Ukrainian immediate family members who were residing in Ukraine prior to 1 January 2022.[53] Children must be accompanied by a parent or guardian, or joining a sponsor approved by the local authority.[54]

On arrival, applicants are granted three years leave to remain and are permitted to work, access education and seek social assistance.

Hong Kong

Hong Kong was a former British colony. Sovereignty was transferred to the People's Republic of China in 1997. The creation of the class of British National (Overseas) was a response to the question of the future prospect for Hong Kong in the 1980s, and therefore the nationality was created for the Hong Kong residents with British Dependent Territories Citizen status by virtue of their connection with Hong Kong. Approximately 3.2 million Hong Kong residents hold the status, which confers protection of the crown, but no right of abode in the UK.

After the Chinese crackdown on dissidents in Hong Kong in 2020, the UK announced it would open a new route for Hong Kong residents with British National (Overseas) passports, to *"reflect the UK's historic and moral commitment to those people of Hong Kong who*

---

[53] Appendix Ukraine

[54] Guidance for Councils: *Homes for Ukraine – Applications to Homes for Ukraine for children who are not travelling or reuniting with their parent or legal guardian*

chose to retain their ties to the UK by taking up BN(O) status before Hong Kong's handover to China in 1997".[55] The scheme launched in January 2021, to create a bespoke route for entry for BN(O) passport holders and their family members to live, work and study in the UK.

The new Appendix Hong Kong British National (Overseas)[56] came into force on 31 January 2021 and had already received thousands of applicants. Principal applicants must be holders of a BN(O) passport, whose ordinary residence is in Hong Kong. They need to provide adequate maintenance for themselves and their dependent family for the first 6 months and not fall foul of the General grounds for Refusal in Part 9 of the Immigration Rules. Applicants may bring with them their dependent partner, minor child or grandchild, and may include dependent adult children or grandchildren who remain part of the household. Other dependent relatives[57] can be included, where they formed a part of the household at the time of application, require assistance as a result of age, illness or disability require long-term personal care to perform everyday tasks, and are unable to get that help in Hong Kong. Applicants must show that they are able to maintain and accommodate themselves without access to public funds for a period of 6 months.[58]

Eligible applicants were initially able to come to the UK via a concession to grant them 'leave outside the rules at the border'. The concession ended on 19 July 2021 and applicants are now required to make an online application for either leave to enter or leave to remain

---

[55] Hong Kong British National (Overseas) Visa policy statement, 22 July 2020

[56] Inserted by HC 813

[57] Defined at HK 48.2 as the parent, grandparent, brother, sister, son or daughter of the BN(O) holder or their partner

[58] The required standard is that of "adequate maintenance" defined in para. 6 to the Immigration Rules

and pay the relevant fee. If successful, applicants will be granted either 30 months or five years leave to remain, depending on the fee paid. Those who were not ordinarily resident at the time of application, or are unable to meet the financial requirements may be granted 12 months leave outside the rules. Leave is normally subject to a no recourse to public funds condition, although applicants may apply to waive that conditions. Applicants will be able to work and study with nor further conditions and may apply to settle after five years.

Syria

The civil unrest in Syria began in March 2011, with an estimated 22 million people affected by the conflict (virtually half of Syria's population). Large numbers spilled over the border, predominantly into Turkey and Lebanon, sparking a huge movement of people across the Middle East and what became known as the European Migrant crisis. The UK, together with many European countries, committed to assisting with durable solutions to relieve the pressure on neighbouring countries.

The Vulnerable Persons Resettlement Scheme

The Syrian Vulnerable Persons Resettlement Scheme (VPRS) was launched in January 2014 and closed to new arrivals on 25 February 2021. The VPRS provided sanctuary to those fleeing the Syrian conflict to neighbouring countries specifically Jordan, Iraq, Lebanon, Turkey and Egypt. The scheme was launched in conjunction with UNHCR with the stated aim of targeting "*those in the greatest need, including people requiring urgent medical treatment, survivors of violence and torture and women and children at risk*".[59] By the time the scheme closed, 20,319 people fleeing the conflict had been resettled in the UK.[60]

As with most resettlement schemes, identification of those in need was done by UNHCR, which then made referrals to the Home Office. Processing time for the referrals was relatively quick, often a matter of weeks and travel documents, funded by the resettled refugee with the help of the IOM, were issued swiftly.[61] On arrival, refugees were allocated to local authorities volunteering to take responsibility for meeting them at the airport, housing them in allocated properties and ensuring ongoing support.

Those arriving were initially granted humanitarian protection rather than refugee status and given leave to remain for five years. In July 2017, the policy changed and those admitted to the UK under the Syrian resettlement scheme are granted immediate refugee status. Both groups are now eligible to apply for ILR.

The Vulnerable Children's Resettlement Scheme

The Vulnerable Children's Resettlement Scheme (VCRS) was launched in 2016, with the aim of resettling up to 3,000 'at-risk' refugee children from the Middle East and North Africa region. The

---

[59] Statement of Prime Minister David Cameron, 7 September 2015, announcing the expanding of the scheme to include those fleeing Syria without Syrian nationality

[60] Immigration Statistics, year ended June 2021 (https://www.gov.uk/government/statistics/immigration-statistics-year-ending-june-2021/how-many-people-do-we-grant-asylum-or-protection-to#data-tables)

[61] Independent Chief Inspector's report: An Inspection of the Vulnerable Persons Resettlement Scheme August 2017-January 2018, published 8 May 2018

scheme targeted both unaccompanied children and those with families, where the children were threatened with child specific forms of exploitation and abuse in the host country. Children and their families were granted five years leave to remain, although are now able to apply for ILR free of charge. Local authorities and partner NGOs provided the families with intensive support, including education, medical and psychological support and one to one support to enable them to integrate into the society in which they were settled. The scheme closed in March 2021, having resettled 1,838 refugees.[62]

The operation of these bespoke routes has met with varied success and reflects the competing political interests at various times. The speed at which the Ukrainian route was rolled out, for example, can be contrasted with the lengthy delays in creating and opening the routes designed for Afghan nationals. The move towards inclusion within Immigration Rules of specific routes is however overall a good approach, largely because it circumvents the delays elsewhere. These routes also allow prospective applicants for resettlement to engage UK based legal teams with experience in domestic immigration law to help them navigate the process. Practical obstacles with access to the various schemes will need to be ironed out, but overall, the increased variety of schemes on offer has improved the UK's commitment to refugee protection.

---

[62] Immigration Statistics, *supra*

CHAPTER FIVE

FAMILY REUNION

Whilst not strictly within the UK's resettlement programs, the family reunion route is the most popular, and best understood, of the legal routes of entry for those in need of international protection. The applicant does not need to be a refugee, and thus many such applications in practice take place without the intervention of UNHCR from the country in which the principal applicant, the family member who has successfully been recognised as refugee in the UK, originates. Nonetheless, in practice, many family members face persecution or ill-treatment of a variety, for similar reasons to that leading to the principal applicants' departure, and thus may be in desperate need of relocation.

Resettlement, as a tool of international protection, involves preserving and restoring the basic dignity of a refugee's life, including promoting the reunification of the refugee's family. This requires that States take measures, including national legislative efforts, to preserve the unity of the family. Family Reunion as a right is absent from the 1951 Geneva Refugee Convention. The Refugee Convention does not include a specific right to family reunion, although the Final Act of the Conference of the Plenipotentiaries which adopted the Convention, declared *"the unity of the family, the natural and fundamental group unit of society, is an essential right of the refugee"*.[63] This declaration has led to many resolutions of the UNHCR

---

[63] Recommendation 'B', Final Act of the United Nations Conference of Plenipotentiaries on the Status of Refugees and Stateless Persons, held at Geneva, Switzerland, From 2 To 25 July 1951

Executive Committee and most regional and national refugee recognition processes now have some form of family reunion program, for those joining family members already recognised as refugees.[64]

In the UK, the route is available to family members of those who have been recognised as refugees, depending on the date on which they were recognised as a refugee, and the manner in which the sponsoring refugee arrived in the UK. Refugees arriving prior to 28 June 2022, whether with five years limited leave to remain or having been granted ILR, may sponsor immediate family members who formed a part of their family prior to leaving to seek asylum. Since 28 June 2022, the UK has operated a two-tier system for refugee recognitions.[65] Those who enter in order to seek asylum, present themselves *"without delay"* to the authorities, and can show *"good cause for their unlawful entry or presence"*, are deemed "Group 1" refugees. Group 1 refugees are permitted to sponsor family reunion applications in the same way as those who arrived before 28 June 2022. "Group 2" refugees, those who do out fulfil each of those criteria, cannot do so. Family members of Group 2 refugees must show that there are insurmountable obstacles to family life continuing without family reunion, or that continued exclusion would otherwise breach the UK's obligations under Article 8 of the European Convention on Human Rights.

The Immigration Rules, at Rules 352A-J, govern family reunion for those eligible. The Rules apply to those who were part of the nuclear family of the refugee, prior to that refugee leaving the country of prior

---

[64] In the European Union, Council Directive 2003/86/EC of 22 September 2003 on the right to family reunification, available at: http://eur-lex.europa.eu/LexUriServ/LexUriServ.do?uri=OJ:L:2003:251:0012:0018:EN:PDF.

[65] S.12 Nationality and Borders Act 2022, brought into force by The Nationality and Borders Act 2022 (Commencement No. 1, Transitional and Saving Provisions) Regulations 2022

habitual residence, in order to seek asylum. This will include a family established in a third country in which the refugee sponsor was living prior to leaving to seek asylum, provided that the sponsor was habitually resident there. Habitually resident is understood to mean *"residence in a place with some degree of continuity and apart from accidental or temporary absences"*[66] and thus can be evidence by those who resided temporarily in a refugee camp, or those who lived and worked in a third country prior to leaving to seek asylum, whether or not the UK was the final envisaged destination. The sponsor must be a refugee living lawfully in the UK, that is they have had their status determined, even if that determination took place outside the UK.[67] This will include those resettled under any of the resettlement schemes. The status must be current – a former refugee who has naturalised as British or whose status has been revoked will no longer be able to sponsor their family members through this route.[68]

Consideration under the Immigration Rules is limited to the spouse, civil partner, unmarried partner – defined as the person with whom the refugee had lived for 2 years in a relationship akin to marriage, and children under the age of 18, provided that they are not living an independent life. This includes adopted children, but only if there is a legal adoption order[69] – although the Rules make provision elsewhere for *de facto* adoptions, those rules expressly do not apply to

---

[66] *Nessa v Chief Adjudication Officer and* another [1999] UKHL 41

[67] *A v Entry Clearance Officer, Pretoria (Somalia)* [2004] UKIAT 00031

[68] Although the Supreme Court in *ZN (Afghanistan) v Entry Clearance Officer* [2010] UKSC 21, [2010] 1 WLR 1275 has held that former refugees were permitted to sponsor family members, the Rules were expressly changed to counter this (by Cm 7944)

[69] A legal adoption order means one the complies with the provisions of the Hague Convention of 29 May 1993 on Protection of Children and Co-operation in Respect of Intercountry Adoption

the family reunion provisions.[70] A child must have been part of the family unit prior to the refugee leaving to seek asylum, and this will include children conceived before the sponsor fled. Any child conceived after that point will not qualify. DNA evidence is not be required as a mandatory qualification, although those who have no other evidence of the relationship may consider obtaining DNA evidence to support the application. Adult children may apply if they can show that there are exceptional circumstances, namely that they are financially and emotionally dependent on one or both of their parents in the UK, there are no other family members providing support and they cannot access other support in the country where they are living and are thus likely to become destitute.[71] Spouses, civil partners and unmarried partners will need to show that their relationship is subsisting and that they intend to live together in the UK. The assessment of whether the relationship is subsisting will have to take account of the fact that the family may have been separated as a result of the persecution that led to the refugee fleeing the country. Those who marry after the refugee sponsor has fled the country may be eligible, provided they met the definition of unmarried partner at the time of the flight. Where the refugee sponsor did not mention the family member on their application for asylum or resettlement, they will need to provide an explanation as to why not, and should expect the application and the attached evidence to be scrutinised very carefully.

Other family members, including children conceived after the refugee fled to seek asylum, will normally be required to meet the relevant provisions of the Immigration Rules, unless a case can be made out that refusing entry clearance on a family reunion application would

---

[70] *AA v Entry Clearance Officer (Addis Ababa)* [2013] UKSC 81, [2014] 1 WLR 43. De facto adopted children must meet the requirements of paras. 309A and 310 of the Immigration Rules

[71] Para 352DB

breach the UK's obligations under the ECHR. The Home Office guidance documents point to a need to assess whether there are insurmountable obstacles to family life continuing without family reunion, or other exceptional or compassionate factors leading to unjustifiably harsh consequences for the applicant or their family.[72] Those applying under Appendix FM will have to show that the sponsor can support and accommodate them, unless they meet the exceptional circumstances provisions of Appendix FM.[73] Cases involving children will have to be considered with their best interests in mind.[74] Consideration will need to factor in the circumstances leading to the family's separation, the conditions in which the applicant is living, their age, cultural considerations and any other support options the applicant might have. Where the need for relocation away from the current situation is urgent, this should be highlighted on the form.

The Immigration Rules do not provide for children recognised as refugees to sponsor their parents or siblings. However, such applications are considered on a case by case basis and parents and siblings of minor persons granted asylum as minors may be granted family reunion if they can show that there are exceptional or compassionate circumstances to do so. The UK courts have made it clear that the absence of a route under the Rules is not to be understood as a blanket prohibition on relatives other than the spouse of minor children of a refugee to be considered in this capacity.[75] Applications should be made using the relevant forms for family reunion and outlining the family's circumstances in full. Decision-

---

[72] API: Family Reunion

[73] Para.3 GEN 3.1 and 3.2

[74] S.55 Borders, Citizenship and Immigration Act 2009

[75] *KF and others (entry clearance, relatives of refugees) Syria* [2019] UKUT 413 (IAC)

makers considering applications from family members of those arriving as unaccompanied minors need to give careful consideration to the strength of the family life, the best interests of the child and the ability of the family to attain its potential.[76]

Family reunion can be applied for directly, without any involvement of UNHCR from the country in which the refugee is based, or the nearest UK visa application point. An application for family reunion is free of charge. The Rules allow for applications to be made from inside or outside the country, including from the country in which the refugee sponsor fears persecution, if that is where family members still live. The process is simpler if made from outside of the country, and is done by completing the online application form, unless the applicant is applying from the Democratic People's Republic of Korea, where the application must be made in person at the British Embassy in Pyongyang. If made in-country, there is no need for a person to have leave to enter or remain at the time they make the application.

Normal maintenance and accommodation requirements to do not apply to applications under the family reunion provisions, although applications considered outside the Rules may be stronger if that support can be shown. The application is subject to certain of the general grounds for refusal in Part 9 of the Immigration Rules and applicants will have to show that they exclusion and criminality thresholds therein. UKVI normally requires that an applicant must enrol their biometrics in order to make a valid application, although the Secretary of State retains a discretion to defer that enrolment until after entry.[77]

---

[76] *AT and another (Article 8 ECHR – Child Refugee – Family Reunification : Eritrea)* [2016] UKUT 227 (IAC)

[77] In *R (on the application of SGW) v Secretary of State for the Home Department (Biometrics , family reunion policy)* [2022] UKUT 15 (IAC), the Upper Tribunal found the API on Family Reunion to be unlawful

Once granted, a family reunion visa is valid for travel within thirty days. If an applicant needs longer to make travel preparations, they should make clear on the application form the earliest date they intend to travel to the UK so that the visa can be issued to start on that day. If the applicant is unable to obtain a passport, they may make an application for a travel document.[78] That will ordinarily be a Convention Travel Document, although in some instances special arrangements will be made to travel on the visa alone.

On entry, or if applied for in-country, the initial grant of leave will be in line with the refugee sponsor. If the refugee sponsor has indefinite leave to remain at the time of entry, the applicant will also be granted indefinite leave. Applicants will not be granted refugee status, unless they themselves undergo an individual assessment. Applicants will be entitled many of the same benefits as a refugee – they will be provided with support to access education and employment, and are entitled to access public funds. They will also be entitled to a Convention Travel Document, subject to the usual criteria. However, since they themselves are not refugees, they will not be entitled to sponsor other family members through the family reunion route – any spouses, children etc will need to meet the requirements of Appendix FM to the Immigration Rules. The travel document and vignette will make clear that they were issued leave as a refugee dependent.

---

insofar as it failed to acknowledge the existence of discretion within the Immigration (Biometric Registration) Regulations 2008 as to the enrolment of biometric information

[78] Para. 344of the Immigration Rules.

CHAPTER SIX

CHALLENGING DECISIONS

Refugee resettlement is separate from the asylum process. As those resettled under the traditional resettlement routes are initially identified as refugees and selected for resettlement by UNHCR, outside of the UK, that process is not immediately governed by domestic law. As such, that stage of the process is not one which can be challenged in the UK. If new information addressing a specific point of refusal, UNHCR may remake the submissions. We set out in Chapter 1 the process for reconsideration and resubmission of applications at that stage. Nonetheless, challenges may be brought against the rejection of a referral by the UK by way of judicial review.

Challenges brought to *ex gratia* schemes, run directly by the UK, as opposed to those run through UNHCR, are more common. Certain schemes brought into the Immigration Rules, attract a statutory route of challenge, which we cover below.

Resettlement under the traditional schemes

The domestic courts have been very clear that their jurisdiction is limited to the construction and application of the UK's policies and practices, not those of UNHCR.[79] If an application is rejected by the

---

[79] *Per* McCombe LJ, *ST & Anor v The Secretary of State for the Home Department* [2014] EWCA Civ 188, at §37. See also *HNA, R (On the Application Of) v Secretary of State for the Home Department* [2021] EWHC 2100 (Admin), where Jacobs J concluded there was no basis for finding

UK as not meeting its criteria or for any other reason, the UK will send a decision letter to UNHCR, briefly outlining the reasons. This is not an immigration decision[80] and therefore there is no right of appeal against that decision. It is however a decision by a public body in the UK, made in accordance with the laws and policies of the UK, and thus is susceptible to judicial review. This does mean that the resettlement schemes and their application are subject to judicial scrutiny to ensure lawful conduct on the part of those designing and applying the schemes.

Challenging the scope or legality of a scheme will be difficult, because the schemes are formulated through the use of prerogative powers, rather than pursuant to any statutory authority.[81] The courts will not step into a political arena, and where a policy is formulated which involves the balance between competing public interests, such as immigration control, economic costs, and international cooperation, the courts will be slow to find a decision is irrational. The Secretary of State, exercising the prerogative powers, has a wide margin of appreciation in determining whether to exercise that power, and what the limits should be.[82] Decisions to impose quotas or to limit schemes to particular geographical areas are political decisions that involve

---

that UNHCR acted as the agent for the UK in the exercise of its functions or that the UK was vicariously liable for the actions of UNHCR staff.

[80] As defined by s.82 Nationality, Immigrating and Asylum Act 2002, as amended

[81] For a useful summary about the limitations on prerogative powers, see *Miller, R (on the application of) v The Prime Minister* [2019] UKSC 41, [2020] AC 373

[82] Per Lords Mance and Carnwath in *Sandiford, R (on the application of) v The Secretary of State for Foreign and Commonwealth Affairs* [2014] UKSC 44, at §65-66. For an application to the resettlement schemes, see *HNA, R (On the Application Of) v Secretary of State for the Home Department* [2021] EWHC 2100 (Admin)

competing political and budgetary interests, and the Courts are not the appropriate place to challenge such decisions. However, the rule of law requires effective access to justice and therefore unless expressly excluded by Parliament, there must be a proper opportunity to challenge an administrative decision.

Procedural unfairness

The rationality of criteria for inclusion within a particular scheme is liable to challenge and criteria must rationally connected to the objective of the policy. [1] In *AK & Ors,*[83] three Iraqi nationals, formerly employed by the British armed forces in Iraq, had fled Iraq in fear of their lives and were recognised by UNHCR as refugees in Syria. They applied under the Iraqi ex gratia scheme, which entitled some former employees to seek relocation to the UK, but were rejected because either they had been employed for less than 12 months, as required by the scheme, or the role was contracted through an agent, rather than as a direct employee. They challenged their exclusion on the basis that the scheme was primarily to recognise the risk that those who worked for the British State, and the imposition of the additional criteria was arbitrary and contrary to the purpose of the scheme. Blake J accepted that if the purpose of the policy had been solely to offer protection to those who were in danger as a result of their employment with the British armed forces, a minimum period of service requirement would have been an irrational. However, he found that the requirement for a former locally engaged employee to have worked for 12 months was

---

[83] In *AK & Ors, R (on the application of) v Secretary of State for Foreign & Commonwealth Affairs & Anor* [2008] EWHC 2227 (Admin). See also *HNA, R (On the Application Of) v Secretary of State for the Home Department* [2021] EWHC 2100 (Admin), where Jacobs J held that the decision not to include a specific category of those who were persecuted on the grounds of religious faith was not irrational, where those individuals were able to access the scheme.

not irrational, because the scheme was expressly not based solely on risk, but rather to reward the length and nature of the relevant employment relationship.

Resettlement schemes must be practically accessible to those who they seek to benefit. Procedures for making applications or representations must be fair and logically reflect the circumstances of the potential applicant; applicants must not be excluded from application to a scheme that they are otherwise eligible for by unnecessary procedural hurdles.[84] The requirement that a resettled refugee complete the biometrics requirement is a rational one, given the security and other needs of the UK, but the requirement to have done so prior to entry is not necessarily so.[85] Forms for applying for consideration under the scheme should accurately reflect the manner in which the application will be processed.[86]

Decisions must always be clearly communicated to the applicant, with reasons that are sufficiently clear for them to ascertain why the application has been rejected. In the *Help Refugees* litigation,[87] the

---

[84] *R (Elias) v Secretary of State for Defence* [2006] EWCA Civ 1293, [2006] 1 WLR 3213. In *S & Anor v Secretary of State for the Home Department & Anor* [2022] EWCA Civ 1092, Underhill LJ found that the failure include an option to waive or defer the obligation to complete the biometrics was irrational, since there was no embassy or VAC in Afghanistan which would permit Afghans to do so.

[85] *KA & Ors, R (On the Application Of) v Secretary of State for the Home Department & Ors* (Rev1) [2022] EWHC 2473 (Admin), *R (on the application of SGW) v Secretary of State for the Home Department (Biometrics , family reunion policy)* [2022] UKUT 15 (IAC)

[86] *S & Anor v Secretary of State for the Home Department & Anor* [2022] EWCA Civ 1092

[87] *Help Refugees Ltd, R (on the application of) v The Secretary of State for Home Department & Anor* [2018] EWCA Civ 2098, [2018] 4 WLR 168. The litigation concerned challenges brought by unaccompanied children refused relocation under section 67 of the Immigration Act 2016, which

Court of Appeal was critical of rejections of those seeking resettlement that simply stated "criteria not met". Given the number of potential criteria, the reasons for rejection were "*patently inadequate*".[88]

Discrimination

Individuals who are in a materially similar position should be treated similarly. A decision to exclude a person from a scheme must not be for unjustifiably discriminatory reasons. The courts will scrutinise carefully decisions which appear to exclude one group of refugees from inclusion within a scheme whilst including another in a similar position. That will involve a careful understanding of the purpose and rationale of the particular scheme, and usually, a comparator group against which comparisons can be made. This will involve obtaining relevant details of the comparator group. Thus, in *R (S) and (AZ)*,[89] Lang J held that a decision to exclude a particular Afghan judge from the ARAP scheme was not discriminatory, since unlike other judges who had been resettled under the scheme, his role had not involved direct contact with the UK's work or made any material contribution to the UK's mission in Afghanistan. However, their exclusion from the Operation Pitting criteria was likely to have been discriminatory, given that thirteen other judges, with no direct or indirect connection

---

committed the UK to make arrangements to relocate and support a specified number of unaccompanied refugee children located in refugee camps elsewhere in Europe. The scheme has since completed.

[88] *Supra*, at §134

[89] *R (S) v Secretary of State for Foreign and Commonwealth and Development Affairs and Ors* and *R (AZ) v Secretary of State for the Home Department and Ors* [2022] EWHC 1402 (Admin), upheld in the Court of Appeal, [2022] EWCA Civ 1092

to the UK's mission had been selected. Conversely, in *SH*,[90] Eyre J felt he was unable to reach a conclusion that the exclusion of certain groups of journalists from the ARAP or LOTR policies was unlawfully discriminatory because of a lack of relevant information about those in the comparator group.

The application of a policy will be subject to the public sector equality duty set out in 149(1) of the Equality Act 2010 (EA 2010).[91] This requires the Secretary of State, as a person concerned in the provision of a service to the public, to ensure that there is no discrimination in the provision of a service to the public, and to remove or minimise disadvantages for those with a protected characteristic.[92] Section 149(7) EA 2010 specifies the relevant protected characteristics for these purposes as age, disability, gender reassignment, pregnancy and maternity, race, religion or belief, sex and sexual orientation. Race is understood to include nationality and national or ethnic origins. In the exercise of "*immigration and nationality*" functions, section 149(1)(b) has effect as if it did not apply to the protected characteristic of race (defined as meaning nationality or ethnic or national origins).[93] In *Turani & Anor*,[94] two Palestinian refugees fleeing conflict in Syria,

---

[90] SH v The Secretary of State for the Home Department [2022] EWHC 1937 (Admin), at §40

[91] *Turani & Anor v Secretary of State for the Home Department* [2021] EWCA Civ 348, approving the judgement of Singh LJ and Carr J in *R (Hoareau and another) v Secretary of State for Foreign and Commonwealth Affairs* [2019] EWHC 221 (Admin), [2019] 1 WLR 4105

[92] SS. 29(1) and 149(1) EA 2010 Act

[93] Para. 2(1) Such 18 EA 2010. Para. 2(2) defines immigration and nationality functions as actions which are exercisable by virtue of the Immigration Acts and other specified legislation concerned with immigration and nationality

[94] *Turani & Anor v Secretary of State for the Home Department* [2021] EWCA Civ 348

were excluded from the VPRS on the basis that they were identified as refugees by UNRWA, not UNHCR. The Court of Appeal held that the protection against discrimination in the provision of services had an extra territorial effect and thus applied to a decision to include or exclude individuals within a scheme. Nonetheless, the discrimination, which was indirect, was justified given the experience of UNHCR and *"the significant degree of trust placed by the United Kingdom Government in UNHCR as uniquely trusted to perform functions that would otherwise have fallen on Government"*,[95] and thus using UNHCR as an exclusive gatekeeper to the scheme was a proportionate means of achieving a legitimate aim.

Decisions under the Immigration Rules

The different routes under the Immigration Rules attract different statutory routes of challenge. Some will attract an appeal right to the First Tier Tribunal automatically, others may have a statutory right to see administrative review. It is important to consider the contents of the applications and the decisions; where a human rights claim has been made and decided, that will also attract a right of appeal.

Family reunion

The rules pertaining to family reunion are expressly considered to invite human rights applications, refusals of which will attract a right of appeal to the First Tier Tribunal.[96] In such cases, an applicant who

---

[95] *Supra,* at §78

[96] S. 82 of the Nationality, Immigration and Asylum Act 2002 determines that a decision to refuse a human rights claim will attract a right of appeal. The Home Office Guidance: *Rights of appeal,* specifies that decisions taken

has been refused entry clearance or leave to remain under the family reunion rules will be able to present their case before an Immigration Judge, together with any further evidence supporting their claim. Such appeals are judged first in line with the immigration rules, but will invite consideration of the wider human rights considerations. Thus, challenges have involved wider family members claiming to fall within the Secretary of State's family reunion policy, whose dependency or position within the family unit is in dispute;[97] children who claim to continue to be a part of the sponsoring refugee family unit;[98] factors to be considered in assessing the circumstances of separation.[99]

Hong Kong British National (Overseas)

Applicants who have been refused leave to remain under Appendix Hong Kong British National (Overseas) are entitled to a right of administrative review.[100] Applications for administrative review may be brought where the applicant considers that the decision-maker has made a case working error; that is that the decision-maker has incorrectly applied the Rules or policy, or wrongly refused the application under Part 9 – general grounds for refusal. This will include challenges based on the lack of evidence, where the decision-maker has failed to request further information in line with the evidential flexibility provisions set out in the policy documents.[101] In

---

under Part 11 of the Immigration Rules, including the provisions governing family reunion, are considered to be human rights appeals.

[97] *Hersi & Ors v Secretary of State for the Home Department* [1996] EWCA Civ 1319

[98] *BM and AL (352D(iv); meaning of "family unit") Colombia* [2007] UKAIT 00055

[99] *Entry Clearance Officer, Addis Ababa v H (Somalia)* [2004] UKIAT 00027

[100] Appendix AR: administrative review, at paras. AR 3.2(g) and AR 5.2(e)

[101] Guidance document: *Hong Kong British National (Overseas) (BN(O)) route*

addition, since the decision-maker has the discretion to consider whether to grant refuse leave outside the rules, the refusal may attract a right of appeal. Where an applicant has made a human rights claim alongside the principal application, and the decision-maker has taken a decision to refuse that human rights claim, the refusal will attract a statutory right of appeal. However, there is no obligation on the decision-maker to make a human rights decision; the Secretary of State is entitled to require that a human rights claim is made separately, using the specific forms.[102]

Ukraine

Decisions taken under the Ukraine Family scheme or the Homes for Ukraine scheme do not attract either a right of appeal or a right to administrative review. There are however no restrictions to the number of times a person or family may apply under the scheme, and therefore the opportunity to correct mistakes or to address concerns raised by the decision-maker is afforded in this way. Applications that are merely resubmitted with no changes are likely to be refused afresh, but the decision-makers are instructed to give full consideration to the application and therefore the opportunity arises to draw attention to any mistakes made in the previous refusal.[103] Decisions under this scheme are processed with relative speed, and therefore in practice, a resubmission is often a quicker route to success.

---

[102] *MY (Pakistan) v Secretary of State for the Home Department* [2021] EWCA Civ 1500, [2022] 1 WLR 238

[103] Guidance document: *Ukraine scheme*

Afghanistan

The decision to refuse an application under Part 7 of the Rules for relocation as a relevant Afghan citizen attracts neither a right of appeal nor access to formal administrative review. However, there is an internal review against refusals under the ARAP scheme, which enables applicants to request a review on grounds that the decision is not in accordance with the policy and to supply further or better evidence where appropriate. That review can normally be requested once only, although the Defence Afghan Relocation and Resettlement team assessing the claim may exceptionally reconsider where there is compelling new evidence.

The ARAP and Ex gratia schemes are complicated, inter-departmental schemes, which are administered by the Secretaries of State for Defence and the Home Office. Decisions to grant or refuse therefore require investigations by both Departments, and where eligibility arises by reason of work with a mission administered by a different department, that department will initially assess eligibility. Challenges to that initial assessment will need to be by way of judicial review, usually of the department making the decision. Applicants will be required to undergo the internal review process first, the outcome of which should produce detailed reasons why the application is being refused.

Leave Outside the Rules

The Secretary of State retains a discretion to grant leave to enter in circumstances not provided for in the Rules (LOTR).[104] The exercise of that power is the subject of formal Home Office guidance.[105] The guidance document specifies that grants should be rare, and decision makers are normally directed to consider applications under the Immigration Rules first, then consider the protections of the ECHR, before considering whether the circumstances are sufficiently compelling or exceptional to warrant a grant of leave outside the Rules. The guidance document specifically recognises that applicants may be those otherwise eligible for one of the resettlement schemes, and encourages applications to be made on the relevant visa application form that most closely matches the applicant's circumstances, not through the resettlement routes. The Court of Appeal in *R(S) and (AZ)* suggested that the requirement to use a form that did not strictly apply to an applicant's circumstances may be irrational given that it would appear to require applicants to falsify certain information in order to proceed, although they were not called upon to make a formal decision to do so in the case before them.[106]

The Court of Appeal has indicated that since there is no obligation to make a resettlement policy, it is difficult to see how Article 8 ECHR is engaged by refusing to admit a person within the terms of that

---

[104] *R (Munir) v Secretary of State for the Home Department* [2012] UKSC 32, [2012] 1 WLR 2192

[105] Guidance document, *Leve Outside the Rules, version 2.0* in force as at date of writing (https://www.gov.uk/government/publications/chapter-1-section-14-leave-outside-the-immigration-rules)

[106] *S & Anor v Secretary of State for the Home Department & Anor* [2022] EWCA Civ 1092, *per* Underhill LJ at §29-30

policy.[107] However, the LOTR policy expressly calls for consideration of human rights principles and compatibility with the ECHR. This potentially opens evidential routes within the challenge. Where the decision maker does take a decision to refuse a human rights claim, that will be a decision that gives rise to a statutory appeal.

Judicial review is not an appeal; it does not normally permit the production of new evidence that was not before the decision-maker at the time of the decision. However, where an application raises grounds suggesting that the decision amounts to a possible breach of rights under the ECHR, the court must make its own assessment and therefore is obliged to take into consideration the new material.[108] That will rarely mean that the reviewing court will take the decision of itself; however, it may direct the Secretary of State to remake the decision, taking the new material into consideration, which may result in a human rights decision being taken.

The courts are slow to interfere with the formulation of a policy, and the decision to include specific criteria. Absent unjustified discrimination, it will largely be a matter for the Secretary of State to determine. Where a policy has been formulated, however, the courts will more readily entertain challenges excluding those who would appear to fall within the policy's rationale, provided that the information provided to the decision-maker enabled them to ascertain that fact. Decision-makers are encourage to ensure that the procedures are fair and reflect the circumstances in which most applicants to the schemes are in. Practitioners are encouraged to ensure that the best

---

[107] Per McCombe LJ, *ST & Anor v The Secretary of State for the Home Department* [2014] EWCA Civ 188

[108] *R (A) v Chief Constable of Kent* [2013] EWCA Civ 1706, *R (BAA) v Secretary of State for the Home Department* [2021] EWCA Civ 1428, [2021] 4 WLR

possible information is available at the earliest stage, and should not be afraid to resubmit applications where better information is available.

CHAPTER SEVEN

FUTURE DEVELOPMENTS

Over the last two years, the UK has revised the asylum system dramatically, and redrawn in particular the resettlement packages on offer. The recent crises in Ukraine and Afghanistan have led to a greater need for understanding of the UK's policies regarding refugees and the global commitments undertaken. Wide-spread support for previous schemes for the resettlement of Syrian refugees and increased calls for safe and legal routes for refugees to gain access to the UK have encouraged the development of policy in this area, and further developments are envisaged over the coming months and years.

Emergency Resettlement Mechanism

In their New Plan for Immigration, the government announced in March 2021 that they would be piloting an urgent procedure "*to enable refugees in urgent need to be resettled more quickly so that life-saving protection is provided in weeks rather than months*".[109] The urgent protection plan, to mirror UNHCR's "Emergency" category, would allow the Secretary of State the power to provide rapid assistance in "*truly and compelling circumstances*".

This program has not yet been rolled out, although the government would argue that the bespoke programs for those from Afghanistan and Ukraine reflect some of the elements of the proposed routes.

---

[109] HM Government, Consultation on New Plan for Immigration: government response, CP 493

Certainly Ukrainian nationals with UK based sponsors have been able to gain access to the scheme, and benefit from a relatively swift relocation package. The ARAP and Afghan Ex gratia scheme, operated in conjunction with the Ministry of Defence, similarly enabled some of those most at risk to access support swiftly, and the emergency evacuation of approximately 15,000 individuals based in Afghanistan in August 2021 reflected several aspect of the proposed procedure. However, the approach has been inconsistent. The increased demand placed on local authorities following both these schemes has meant that a proposed pilot urgent procedure, to be run in conjunction with UNHCR from autumn 2021, was put on hold.[110] However, it is hoped that a bespoke urgent procedure route will be opened in the near future. Any such urgent procedure will need to be identifiable to UNHCR, and ensure that local authorities have both adequate housing stock and the funding to provide for the assistance needed in such cases.

Routes for Skilled refugees

Many refugees seeking resettlement are capable of filling much needed skills gaps in the UK. However, as a result of either their status in the host country, lack of access to appropriate application centres or inability to confirm their linguistic or other skills through the specified documentary requirements, they are unable to apply for work in the UK under the various points-based routes. Lengthy delays in the asylum system in the UK, coupled with the inability to access relevant professional education, leads to many with skills sorely needed by the UK unable to utilise those skills for long periods after entry.

---

[110] Statement of Kevin Foster, then Parliamentary Under-Secretary of State for the Home Department, to Parliament on 2 March 2022

In July 2021, the UK announced that it would runs a Displaced Talent Mobility pilot, run in conjunction with the NGO, Talent Beyond Boundaries,[111] aimed at skilled Syrian refugees resident in Lebanon and Jordan.[112] Rather than a stand-alone route of entry, it is better understood as a tailored version of the Skilled Work visa, allowing employers to hire refugee candidates. Applicants must meet the normal requirements, be able to speak English, have a job offer and prove that they have the necessary skills to fulfil roles on the UK's Shortage Occupation List. Engineers and IT experts are particularly targeted for the scheme. As subset of the scheme, the International Refugee Healthcare pilot, aims to support health and care trained refugees obtain Health and Care Visas, aimed particularly at recruiting nursing staff. As with other applicants to the Skilled Worker route, applicants are able to bring immediate dependent family members.

Applicants receive priority processing, and practical support from Talent Beyond Boundaries, working directly with the case working team to assist with administrative barriers, employment references, and tax records. Successful applicants will have access to safeguards in the event that they lose their job to ensure they are not returned to a country where they may face danger. As with other international skilled workers, candidates will be entitled to a five year Skilled Worker Visa, with the possibility of settlement if the job offer remains in place.

The pilot schemes, due to run for one to two years, have thus far proven popular with both employers and refugees. The UK has confirmed that these pilots will not form part of the overall resettlement numbers, when they are fixed. The projected numbers are relatively low, the pilots aim to offer places to between 100-150

---

[111] For details of the scheme and how to access it, see
https://www.talentbeyondboundaries.org/knowledge-centre

[112] Statement of Priti Patel, then Home Secretary, on 19 July 2021

people and their families. Similar projects in Canada[113] and Australia[114] have thus far proven successful, although are equally in the pilot phase and thus implementation costs are not known. Such programs will never be a replacement for traditional resettlement routes, excluding as they do large numbers of those more urgently in need. However, as both a representation of the potential benefits hosting refugees can bring to the UK and a complementary program allowing skilled refugees to use and develop their skills, these programs can provide a welcome durable solution for the small numbers involved.

Routes for Channel Migrants

Many NGOs and other stakeholders have called for "safe and legal routes" for migrants who make the journey across Europe and wish to come to the UK, highlighting the risks taken by those aiming to come to the UK and the growth in human trafficking.[115] Successive governments have resisted those calls, suggesting that those travelling by "irregular" means are somehow "jumping the queue". During the passage of the Nationality and Borders Act 2022, parliamentarians

---

[113] The Economic Mobility Pathways Pilot (https://www.canada.ca/en/immigration-refugees-citizenship/services/refugees/economic-mobility-pathways-pilot.html)

[114] The skilled migration program (https://immi.homeaffairs.gov.au/what-we-do/skilled-migration-program/recent-changes/skilled-refugee-labour-agreement-pilot-program)

[115] See, for example Migration Observatory, press release, 'A tale of two protection systems: Afghan refugees turn to small boats while Ukrainians use "safe and legal routes" to reach UK', 25 August 2022; Home Affairs Committee, Channel crossings, migration and asylum, 18 July 2022; Joint Council for the Welfare of Immigrants, Safe and Legal Routes of Entry to the UK, 12 August 2020; Foreign Affairs Committee, Responding to irregular migration: a diplomatic route, HC 107, 4 November 2019

considered an amendment which would have provided a legal route of entry to the UK for unaccompanied children and certain other migrants in Europe with relatives in the UK.[116] The provision would have enabled eligible individuals to enter the UK to claim asylum. It was initially approved by the Lords but was rejected by the Commons. The Home Affairs Committee recommended the piloting of safe and legal routes alongside other measures deterring irregular cross-Channel migration as part of its two-year inquiry into Channel crossings, migration and asylum.[117]

With the withdrawal from the European Union on 31 December 2020, the UK lost access to the Dublin III procedure, which allowed European States, including the UK, and individual refugees and asylum-seekers, routes for safe transfer across Europe, according to fixed and known criteria. Although the UK was a net receiver of asylum-seekers and refugees in the final five years of its EU membership, Home Office data shows that consistent numbers of requests were sent in both directions, allowing for safe and legal movements across Europe.[118] Attempts to negotiate replacement bilateral agreements continue, and may give rise to new routes for the lawful entry of refugees and asylum-seekers in need.

---

[116] See sections 4 and 5 of House of Commons Library briefing Nationality and Borders Bill: Progress of the Bill, CBP 9386

[117] Home Affairs Committee, Channel crossings, migration and asylum, 18 July 2022

[118] Asylum and resettlement datasets – Dublin Regulation, published 25 February 2021

Conclusion

The global refugee population continues to grow, placing increasing pressure on the refugee system, particularly in countries neighbouring conflict zones. Long-term, durable solutions are needed to provide support for those most in need, and to assist host countries absorb and share the burden of hosting large refugee populations. Resettlement continues to be one of the solutions best suited for certain groups of refugees, and allows host States to feel supported by the global community.

The international refugee resettlement program is now well-established through the program that UNHCR has run in a similar fashion for several decades. The UNHCR resettlement handbook, first published in 1996, was last revised in 2011, although the country chapters have since been updated.[119] It reflects a hope that more countries would increase and solidify resettlement programs, and a desperation that not enough places were available worldwide. In its annual report, *Projected Global Resettlement Needs 2022*, UNHCR identified the growing need for durable solutions, particularly in Europe and the Americas, as a result of the conflicts in the regions. Africa remained the region in greatest need of resettlement opportunities, as a result of the perpetually high numbers as a result of the protracted refugee situations on the continent.[120] The report, written before the war in Ukraine began, noted that nearly 40 percent

---

[119] UNHCR Resettlement Handbook and Country Chapters, last updated in April 2018

[120] UNHCR: *Projected Global Resettlement Needs 2022*, (https://www.unhcr.org/uk/protection/resettlement/60d320a64/projected-global-resettlement-needs-2022-pdf.html), accessed 4 November 2022.

of all global resettlement cases were submitted to Canada and Sweden, with the UK amongst the top ten countries of resettlement.[121]

By mid-2022, the number of those resettled had risen dramatically, with more than 43,000 refugees from over 70 countries, officially resettled through UNHCR programs in the first six months of the year.[122] However, over a similar period, those requiring resettlement rose at a greater speed. The *Projected Global Resettlement Needs 2023* report[123] noted the growing resettlement needs as refugee numbers rose significantly, placing enormous pressures on host countries bordering conflict zones and countries experiencing dire humanitarian crises. The report also highlighted an increased need for safe pathways for refugees, and advocates strongly that resettlement countries set aside specific quotas for those deemed as in need of urgent or emergency need.

Several European countries have now created or expanded community sponsorship schemes, highlighting the potential benefits and challenges of the schemes.[124] The European Commission has financed a program called SAFE – "*foSter cooperAtion For improving access to*

---

[121] UNHCR: *Global resettlement statistical report*

[122] UNHCR: *Mid-Year Trends, 2022,* published 27 October 2022

[123] UNHCR: *Projected Global Resettlement Needs 2022,* (https://www.unhcr.org/uk/publications/brochures/62b18e714/2023-projected-global-resettlement-needs.html), accessed 4 November 2022

[124] See for example United Nations High Commissioner for Refugees report: *A study on the potential for introducing a community sponsorship program for refugees in Sweden: Scoping report prepared for UNHCR's Representation for the Nordic and Baltic Countries* (https://www.unhcr.org/neu/wp-content/uploads/sites/15/2020/12/UNHCR-Study-on-Community-Sponsorship-Program-in-Sweden.pdf) and European Commission report: *Spain: Pilot programme for the reception and integration of refugees* (https://ec.europa.eu/migrant-integration/news/spain-pilot-programme-reception-and-integration-refugees_en)

protEction", aimed at encouraging cooperation between organisations supporting sponsorship systems and complementary pathways for identified refugees. Individual European countries have increased the pathways available, whether through formal resettlement schemes or *ad hoc* programs aimed at assisting with particular crises. However, despite high level talks with aim of achieving greater burden and responsibility sharing through the region, there remain no settled European wide resettlement schemes.

In recent years the UK has become one of the largest contributors to the global refugee resettlement program. The UK's new UKRS allows in principle for a far greater flexibility than its predecessors; it is not tied to any particular conflict or region, and thus is capable of being responsive to new resettlement needs as they arise. The UK has also proven that where there is a political will, new situation-specific situations can be drawn up to reflect an emergent need – the Ukraine schemes were launched within days of the Russian invasion of Ukraine. Better knowledge of the Community Sponsorship scheme and the Mandate scheme will also lead to an increased ability for the UK population to participate in the resettlement directly, alleviating some of the burden from government departments.

The family reunion scheme, which is by far the most used of the routes examined by this book, is increasingly accessible, with clear criteria, and allows individuals to make direct representations, with proper judicial oversight of the operation. However, other than the schemes run under the Immigration Rules, access to the resettlement schemes remains difficult and opaque. The UK current operates no urgent procedure, and thus those most urgently in need are currently not welcomed through any scheme. It remains unclear what numbers the UK has committed to under the UKRS, and the lack of formal commitment makes it difficult to predict the trends in coming years. That commitment will depend on local authority capacity, and willing, to accept resettled refugee.

In practice, access to these schemes will largely depend on identification by UNHCR and working with UNHCR in host countries to secure referrals. Resettlement continues to be available to a very small percentage of those recognised as refugees outside their countries of origin. Nonetheless, knowledge of the routes available to refugee families, including those that fall outwith the traditional resettlement sphere, can only benefit practitioners and individuals alike.

MORE BOOKS BY
LAW BRIEF PUBLISHING

A selection of our other titles available now:-

'A Practical Guide to Parental Alienation in Private and Public Law Children Cases' by Sam King QC & Frankie Shama
'Contested Heritage – Removing Art from Land and Historic Buildings' by Richard Harwood QC, Catherine Dobson, David Sawtell
'The Limits of Separate Legal Personality: When Those Running a Company Can Be Held Personally Liable for Losses Caused to Third Parties Outside of the Company' by Dr Mike Wilkinson
'A Practical Guide to Transgender Law' by Robin Moira White & Nicola Newbegin
'Artificial Intelligence – The Practical Legal Issues (2nd Edition)' by John Buyers
'A Practical Guide to Residential Freehold Conveyancing' by Lorraine Richardson
'A Practical Guide to Pensions on Divorce for Lawyers' by Bryan Scant
'A Practical Guide to Challenging Sham Marriage Allegations in Immigration Law' by Priya Solanki
'A Practical Guide to Legal Rights in Scotland' by Sarah-Jane Macdonald
'A Practical Guide to New Build Conveyancing' by Paul Sams & Rebecca East
'A Practical Guide to Defending Barristers in Disciplinary Cases' by Marc Beaumont
'A Practical Guide to Inherited Wealth on Divorce' by Hayley Trim
'A Practical Guide to Practice Direction 12J and Domestic Abuse in Private Law Children Proceedings' by Rebecca Cross & Malvika Jaganmohan
'A Practical Guide to Confiscation and Restraint' by Narita Bahra QC, John Carl Townsend, David Winch
'A Practical Guide to the Law of Forests in Scotland' by Philip Buchan
'A Practical Guide to Health and Medical Cases in Immigration Law' by Rebecca Chapman & Miranda Butler
'A Practical Guide to Bad Character Evidence for Criminal Practitioners by Aparna Rao
'A Practical Guide to Extradition Law post-Brexit' by Myles Grandison et al

'A Practical Guide to Equity Release for Advisors' by Paul Sams
'A Practical Guide to Financial Services Claims' by Chris Hegarty
'The Law of Houses in Multiple Occupation: A Practical Guide to HMO Proceedings' by Julian Hunt
'Occupiers, Highways and Defective Premises Claims: A Practical Guide Post-Jackson – 2nd Edition' by Andrew Mckie
'A Practical Guide to Financial Ombudsman Service Claims' by Adam Temple & Robert Scrivenor
'A Practical Guide to Advising Schools on Employment Law' by Jonathan Holden
'A Practical Guide to Running Housing Disrepair and Cavity Wall Claims: 2nd Edition' by Andrew Mckie & Ian Skeate
'A Practical Guide to Holiday Sickness Claims – 2nd Edition' by Andrew Mckie & Ian Skeate
'Arguments and Tactics for Personal Injury and Clinical Negligence Claims' by Dorian Williams
'A Practical Guide to Drone Law' by Rufus Ballaster, Andrew Firman, Eleanor Clot
'A Practical Guide to Compliance for Personal Injury Firms Working With Claims Management Companies' by Paul Bennett
'RTA Allegations of Fraud in a Post-Jackson Era: The Handbook – 2nd Edition' by Andrew Mckie
'RTA Personal Injury Claims: A Practical Guide Post-Jackson' by Andrew Mckie
'On Experts: CPR35 for Lawyers and Experts' by David Boyle
'An Introduction to Personal Injury Law' by David Boyle

These books and more are available to order online direct from the publisher at www.lawbriefpublishing.com, where you can also read free sample chapters. For any queries, contact us on 0844 587 2383 or mail@lawbriefpublishing.com.

Our books are also usually in stock at www.amazon.co.uk with free next day delivery for Prime members, and at good legal bookshops such as Wildy & Sons.

We are regularly launching new books in our series of practical day-to-day practitioners' guides. Visit our website and join our free newsletter to be kept informed and to receive special offers, free chapters, etc.

You can also follow us on Twitter at www.twitter.com/lawbriefpub.

Printed by BoD"in Norderstedt, Germany